HAROLD LLOYD'S
WORLD OF COMEDY

By William Cahn

Einstein: A Pictorial Biography
The Laugh Makers: A Pictorial History
of American Comedians
The Jazz Age *(with Marvin Barrett)*
The Story of Pitney-Bowes
Good Night, Mrs. Calabash: The Secret
of Jimmy Durante
The Story of Writing *(with Rhoda Cahn)*
Harold Lloyd's World of Comedy

"A short time ago, I walked out of my hotel and the usual bunch of autograph kids were hanging around.

"As I signed a few books, a little girl of twelve or so came rushing up. One of her friends yelled to her:

"'That's Harold Lloyd!'

"'Who is he?' she yelled back.

"'He's a comedian, you dope,' her friend said."

HAROLD LLOYD'S
WORLD OF COMEDY

BY WILLIAM CAHN

DUELL, SLOAN AND PEARCE
NEW YORK

First edition

 *Affiliate of*
MEREDITH PRESS
Des Moines & New York

Library of Congress Catalogue Card Number: 64-12440
Manufactured in the United States of America for Meredith Press

CONTENTS

9

10

Introduction

What makes people laugh?

Many things—of course.

What is funny at one time and place may be soberly serious —even somber—at another.

But there are certain laugh-provoking situations and antics that appear to be timeless. The downfall of false dignity is one. The confrontation of fraud with the reality of fact (pomposity slipping on a banana peel) is perpetually funny to most people.

Moreover, visual comedy has proven a reliable laugh-provoker through all time and in all languages, especially in the movies. And no era has supplied more guffaws per minute than what is referred to nostalgically as the Golden Age of Comedy in motion pictures—roughly a period from 1912 to 1932.

11

When it comes to comedy, we are all experts. But even among experts, few people are so well qualified to talk about comedy as Harold Lloyd. He is the comedian about whom James Agee, the critic, wrote: "If plain laughter is any criterion, few people have equaled him, and nobody has ever beaten him."

More than that. Ever since pictures in America first learned to move, he has been one of the nation's most thoughtful students of comedy.

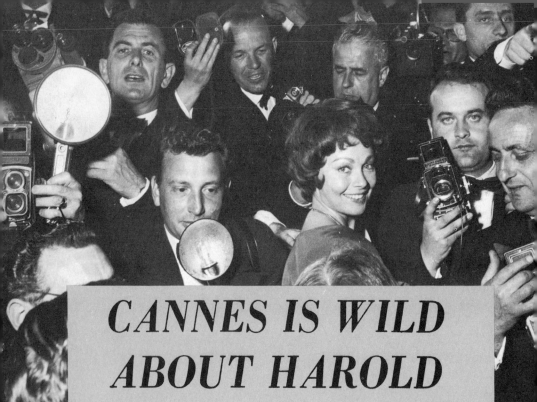

CANNES IS WILD ABOUT HAROLD

CANNES (France), May 12. — (UPI) — The biggest hit of the Cannes Film Festival thus far·has been a movie which began 40 years ago.

And its star, a graying, mild-mannered man who has not made a movie in 30 years, has been wildly cheered by the festival audiences.

Harold Lloyd, one of America's greatest comedians, showed the film — a collection of clips from eight of his most popular silent and sound movies beginning with "The Freshmen" (1925) to "Movie Crazy" (1932).

Lloyd scored what is considered by observers here the biggest single-handed triumph in the star-studded festival. Crowds cheered him with the kind of enthusiasm usually reserved for screen beauties like Sophia Loren and Natalie Wood.

A capacity crowd saw the movie, "Harold Lloyd's World of Comedy," the only film thus far which has been repeatedly applauded throughout its showing.

After it was finished Lloyd, who sat in the balcony, was given a huge ovation and the crowd then poured out into the street to cheer him off.

Lloyd said the movie would be released next month in the United States and Europe.

Harold Lloyd's World of Comedy was presented to the motion picture audiences of the world in 1962. It was an anthology of sequences—some silent and some talking—from a selection of famous Lloyd movies. The film was launched before a special showing at the Cannes Film Festival in France.

Perhaps it was nostalgia. Or perhaps the audience of exhibitors, entertainers, correspondents, and writers from dozens of nations had enough of grim debauches, tormented souls, and bare bosoms for that day.

At any event, Lloyd's film was like a cool breeze to feverish brows.

What began perhaps as a polite salute to a favorite of yesterday turned into a continuous explosion of uproarious laughter. Harold Lloyd's ability to rush from one gag to another, his once well-known knack of building from laugh to laugh, seemed to work today as well as generations before.

After it was all over, the sixty-eight-year-old comedian—seated apprehensively in the audience—was accorded a standing ovation.

"It was a response," said Harold, "far beyond my fondest dreams."

15

Will the man who made Dad laug make you laugh too?

A KEYSTONE comic called Harold Lloyd—tired of aping Chaplin with a moustache, baggy pants and small hat—bought a pair of horn-rimmed spectacles from a Los Angeles optician, knocked out the lenses to avoid re-fl... ....dio lights. put on a straw boater

By PAUL DEHN,
Daily Herald film critic

which had not been rolled in since the Columbia was built.

It is not merely the period properties which impel our laughter, though slapstick was never to be the same again after the dis- ...m ....ary sc....

The *London Daily Herald* wondered in bold headlines if the Harold Lloyd brand of humor was still potent. The *London Mirror* came to the conclusion that it definitely was. After seeing a preview of Lloyd's picture, an editor of *Life* magazine asked, "Whatever happened to all that old-time laughter that exploded in the belly, roared up through the ribs and fizzed out in snorts and chortles? Well, it's having a comeback."

Bosley Crowther of *The New York Times* described the *World of Comedy* as "a joy and a delight in this sad world."

"Lloyd's best stuff is still terribly funny, much funnier than anything we have today," said John Crosby in the *Washington*

16

ES..THEY DO LAUGH AT THOSE OLD FILM GAGS

ANDRA laughed. The middle-aged critics roared.
t what would the youngsters of today think of the films
hirty years ago by American comedian Harold Lloyd?
rday the Mirror took seventeen youngsters to see
" World of Comedy," a selection from
the best of Lloyd's comedies.

They watched Lloyd becoming involved with —
among other things—a live turkey in a crowded
bus; a wild car chase; a Mexican revolution; a
runaway tram; and a window cleaner's cradle
halfway up a skyscraper.

the lights went up after the show—in the
ma at the May Fair Hotel, London—the
what they thought . . .
ful Baker twins, 16-year-old
impressed.
prefer the more

VERDICT

It was really funny.
And so OLD, too. I
suppose I'm just a
girl who likes slap-
stick after all.

— Susan· Maug-
ham, 19, cabaret
singer, of New-
castle - upon -
Tyne.

VERDICT

Excellent. Especially
those traffic scenes
with the old cars
ust missing each
her. How did they
it?

— Barry Gray,
18, insurance
ffice trainee,
Sydenham,

Post. The *Motion Picture Daily* warned exhibitors to "note while planning to accommodate the extra crowds at the box office, that critics and columnists have been unanimous in delighted praise."

Laughing at Harold Lloyd was not exactly a new custom. Back almost half a century, it was one of the most enjoyable occupations for millions of people. Around 1917, a young man in search of a comedy character that would not borrow from the great Charlie Chaplin, purchased a pair of horn-rimmed glasses and set himself up seriously in the laugh-making business.

17

Without competition from radio or television, motion pictures were then the most widely liked formal entertainment. Soon the name of Harold Lloyd became a symbol for laughter throughout the world. His following grew to such numbers that motion picture houses in some communities did not dare advertise the coming of Harold Lloyd's movies when they arrived in town, so great was the outpouring.

By 1926, *The New Yorker* magazine was describing him as "the most affluent and popular of all the stars in the Hollywood heavens."

There were more substantial rewards for Harold than popularity. His motion picture successes made him into a millionaire

many times over. "Lloyd's gross take of more than thirty million dollars," commented *Newsweek* magazine in 1941, "is probably a record for any performer."

Hollywood was a golden city in those days before the discovery of the income tax, and Harold showed a precocious ability both to make dollars and hold on to them.

Even rarer was his knack of keeping his nimble feet in contact with the earth. Despite the fact that he was established, as one newspaper put it, "as the highest-priced actor in the world," he displayed an almost disappointing modesty. Robert E. Sherwood, the famous playwright, who was then a movie critic, described Lloyd as "unquestionably the most unexpected, the most thoroughly improbable occupant of the gilded picture frame of success. For he is painfully devoid of all the blatancy, all the splurge that goes with achievement in this nation, and more particularly on the screen."

There is scarcely another celebrity within memory who made as much money as Lloyd, saved as much; married and stayed married to the same woman as long; and generally conducted himself so consistently as a normal human being.

When the Academy of Motion Picture Arts and Sciences sought a recipient for a special Oscar in 1952, it selected Lloyd and inscribed upon the statuette: "Master Comedian and Good Citizen."

Today, Lloyd has a set of strong opinions concerning comedy, past and present. In the first place, he is convinced of the importance of laugh-making for the health of this country, and the world. But he is not so sure that modern comedy is performing its function as it should. "Comedy is different today," he says. "Laughs come mostly from wisecracks, puns, insult humor, kidding around, smart lines, and so on. What we call intellectual jokes. You have to know your English pretty well to laugh at them at all.

"But our comedy of years ago was international—in China, Timbuctoo or Boston. Our gags got yaks and everybody was happy.

"People nowadays ask me how it is that my comedies seem to get as big laughs from audiences now as they did when they were first made. My answer is that comedy that is basic will live forever. It can't be impaired by sound, color, wide screens or any other development in the film medium.

"How were our comedies made? Was it luck or science? How did we get the gags that have lasted for so long and are still funny?

"People are still asking me about my world of comedy."

Harold Lloyd in the early silent motion picture *Damon and Pythias*.
Lloyd is in the middle of the back group. To his right is another
extra, the famous comedy movie producer Hal Roach.

22

CHAPTER ONE

The Making of a Comedian

"My ambition to be an actor goes back to the first time I can remember knowing what an actor was," said Harold Lloyd. "I never had any other idea.

"As a boy, I was simply crazy to act. Ours was not a theatrical family and, so far as I know, no one connected with it has ever been in the theater. The little town in Nebraska where I was born was a long way from Broadway. There was no theater and no opportunity for a youngster to build an interest in the entertainment world.

"Nevertheless, the bug bit me early. And when my family moved around, as it did frequently, I began to play in amateur theatricals. Not comedy, mind you. But any type of acting where I could get near grease paint and footlights. When I was only twelve years old, I was playing Little Abe in *Tess of the D'Urbervilles*."

A sign near the birthplace of Harold Lloyd in Nebraska.

Put a finger on what you would consider the central point of the United States; you will not be far from Burchard, Nebraska, where Harold Clayton Lloyd was born on April 20, 1893. He was the second of two sons of James D. Lloyd and his wife, the former Sarah E. Fraser.

The Lloyd clan moved west from Pennsylvania in the late 1800's and settled in the home territory of the Pawnee Indians. At the time of Harold's arrival, Burchard consisted of little more than half a dozen stores, a school, and two churches.

The elder Lloyd (nicknamed "Foxy") was a photographer who frequently moved his family about in search of work. Schooling for the children was thus often interrupted. But certain teachings of the period sank in, mostly based on such texts as the *McGuffey's Readers*. The Lloyd boys were impressed with the importance of certain virtues, such as self-reliance, determination, dependability, thrift, and the triumph of justice over all obstacles. Years later these teachings were to influence Harold's motion-picture character, but in a manner scarcely predictable in the early years.

"I was average," recalls Lloyd, "and typical of the time and place. I might have been "Master America" most any year between 1893 and 1910. This is assuming that the average boy before the war was moderately poor, that his folks moved a good deal, and that he worked for his spending money at any job offered.

"As to ambition, I cannot remember ever wanting to be an engineer, fireman, policeman, bakery-wagon driver, or any of

24

the other career goals of boys. As far back as memory goes, and to the exclusion of all else, I was stage-crazy. There is no accounting for the dream's strength and persistence, for it began before I ever saw a play, and there were no actors, so far as we know, in either my father's or my mother's family.

"Even as a little boy, I was crazy about makeup. I remember how I would spend hours before the mirror making eyebrows and mustaches with charcoal or anything that would leave a mark on my small face. Then I experimented on all the boys in the neighborhood. We would dress up in all sorts of wild costumes and prance up and down the quiet streets."

Harold's first actual stage appearance was in the village of Beatrice, Nebraska, where he played the part of Fleance, Banquo's ill-fated son in Shakespeare's *Macbeth*, in a local repertory company. In this part, Harold merely appeared, cried "Help!" and exited running.

Harold Lloyd as a young man whose ambition was to become a dramatic actor.

25

Harold Lloyd nursed ambitions to become a professional boxer until his mother put her foot down.

"Only once did my desire to go on the stage lapse, and that was in one of the five high schools in different cities that I attended. A fondness for gym work turned my thoughts to prize-fighting. I appeared in the ring several times.

"The name Harold used to be—maybe is yet—in low repute with kids. It was supposed to be sissy, and its possessors frequently had to defend it with their fists. I picked up a few rudiments of boxing very early, therefore, and was several jumps ahead of the average boy my age.

"I thought seriously of taking up fighting professionally. I always have been fast and shifty, and I had sold my mother on the idea that it was good for a boy to know the manly art or self-defense. However, when she heard that I was considering boxing as a career, she put her foot down."

26

When Harold Lloyd was seventeen, his father moved the family to San Diego, California, where he purchased a pool hall and lunch counter—"Don't ask me why," says Lloyd.

Harold attended high school, helped his father at work, played in school shows, and portrayed various characters, mostly villains, for local stock companies. He also gave Shakespeare readings before high school English classes and worked as a stage hand at a local theater. "And all simultaneously," says Harold.

"I had an enormous advantage over my schoolmates when it came to acting. But I came near losing my head in the process." The guidance of John Lane Connor, a local stock company producer who had known the Lloyd family back in Nebraska, was of importance to Harold throughout this period.

"Back in the winter of 1912, our high school had given a collegiate farce in which I played the leading man. During the opening performance, one of the performers' nose began to bleed copiously. He had to walk off the stage, leaving me to conduct a monologue. And I got away with it.

"The next morning, I drifted into the school anticipating praise. But Mr. Connor seemed unimpressed. I stood about waiting for it, but it didn't come. 'I wasn't so bad last night, was I?' I asked.

"I remember Connor hesitating, as if reluctant to be involved in so painful a discussion. Then he answered quietly:

"'Harold, I was very much disappointed in you last night. After all, you're not an amateur in his first play. But I wouldn't have known that last night. You pulled yourself out of a hole very well. But why shouldn't you? You've been working at the trade for years.

"'On the other hand, how many times have I told you how to get the full value out of a laugh? Of course, you got laughs. The laughs were in the lines and situations. Half the time, though, you choked them to death before they were started.'

"As I remember it, Connor went over my performance point by point, as a mechanic goes over a motor, pointing out bad timing, wrong emphasis, and other errors in technique. I have never forgotten this incident. Not only was I brought down

out of the clouds with a thud which I deserved, but I was taught important techniques of comedy, of spacing, of timing, which have remained a permanent part of my comic vocabulary throughout my career."

This was an era when motion pictures were just getting started. The West Coast was proving an ideal locale for outdoor picture-taking the year around. "Actually, I stumbled into pictures," says Harold. "It was a stopgap to fill a hungry stomach. I went into pictures only because they were on hand in California, and nothing else offered.

"When the old Edison Company of New York came to San Diego on location, it was the first motion picture company I ever saw in my life. I became fired with the ambition every kid then had—of getting into the movies."

Young Lloyd's ability at make-up proved useful to him in the early days of motion pictures. *Left,* Harold Lloyd whispering sinister words to the famous matinee idol of the day, J. Warren Kerrigan.

August
22
1938

The Harold Lloyd Studios
Hollywood, California

Dear Sirs:

    Members of the student body at San Diego
High School consider Mr. Harold Lloyd as perhaps
the most successful graduate of our school. We
are glad to hear from him at frequent intervals
and are more pleased to attend his motion pictures
when they are released. His last--"Professor
Beware"--topped all others that we may remember
and we are proud of the success.

    Because of these facts, I am asking if we
may obtain an autographed picture of Mr. Lloyd
for the Associated Student Body office. We
would greatly appreciate this courtesy and sin-
cerely hope that it is not too great a bother
for you or Mr. Lloyd. We realize, of course,
the busy life which Mr. Lloyd lives.

    With many thanks and best wishes, I am,

Truly yours,

Charles Wallis, President
3875 Superba Street
San Diego, California

One day in the late spring of 1912, the company was shooting a picture requiring the assistance of a group of extras dressed up as Indians. Harold Lloyd volunteered, made up as a naked Yaqui, and served a tray of food in a brief scene. The pay was three dollars a day.

This was Harold's debut in motion pictures, and other small bit parts were to follow. Wherever extras were needed, Harold applied. In one picture, he had a tiny part in a barn dance. When the film was shown at a ten-cent motion picture house in town, Harold went to see himself for the first time.

"My vanity never took a worse wallop than when I saw how I looked on the screen. The shock that comes with the first glance at the proofs a photographer mails you after the sitting is something like it. None of us photographs as he imagines himself, and of the two likenesses, the camera's is not the flattering one. I was disgusted with the movies. But nothing else offered at the moment."

In 1913, Harold's father went job hunting in Los Angeles, the actual center of the new motion picture industry, located near the rapidly expanding Hollywood center. Harold was delighted. As soon as he graduated from San Diego High School, he followed his father and immediately sought employment as a moving picture extra.

But jobs were hard to find. Weeks passed without work.

"I met with resistence and discouragement at every stage. I could not even get past a studio gate. Finally I did—at Universal. After days of waiting there, one day I put on make-up in back of a little restaurant across from the studio gate and, after the lunch period, mingled with the crowd of extras, slipped past the gate man, and got inside the studio for the first time."

Once inside, Harold waited for casting roles. They were slow to come. But come they did. Finally, Harold was in movies—serious movies. Not until later did he learn that, in another part of Los Angeles, strange things were happening involving fake policemen, bathing girls who never went near the water, and acrobats who were referred to as comedians.

CHAPTER TWO

The Laugh Factories

While Harold Lloyd was involved in San Diego High School dramatics, the first Keystone comedy was being produced about 120 miles away on a vacant lot in the sprawling city of Los Angeles.

Early film comedies were the products of several pioneers. First was Mack Sennett, master of the Keystone pictures, followed by Hal Roach, the Christie Brothers, and others. These early laugh-makers realized the potential of the new industry in the specialized area of comedy; and set about to make America—and all the world—laugh as it had never laughed before.

Sennett was a huge, bearlike man, a rough-and-tumble

Comedies frequently involved sheriffs, dogs, and trains. *Left,* Wallace Beery, on the tracks, with Gloria Swanson among those present.

former boiler maker with experience in the circus, burlesque, and vaudeville. "Had he done nothing else," says Harold Lloyd, who was a Sennett employee briefly in the early days, "Mack Sennett would be remembered today as the man who did more to make the world laugh than any other single individual in the history of films."

It was under Roach, however, that Lloyd obtained his real start as one of the world's great comedy stars. "Roach was an extremely creative man," says Lloyd. "He had a mind that drew ideas seemingly out of thin air. He was not always the one to develop these ideas, but he had the good sense to encourage initiative in others once he had started them on their way."

Like Sennett, Roach was a big man, strong and energetic. Both Sennett and Roach had an earthy spirit, an intuitive feeling about what makes laughs. Roach had gone west from Elmira, New York, as a youth. He had drifted through the Pacific Northwest up to Alaska and back to Southern California. In 1913, he met Harold Lloyd on the Universal Studios' lot, where both were working as extras.

"Those were the days when movies were in their infancy, and people were experimenting with the infinite opportunities that the film medium offered for comedy," says Lloyd. "They were able to do things that simply weren't possible on the stage, in circuses or in any other medium."

Sennett and Roach, more than anyone else, helped usher in the Golden Age of Comedy in the movies. Throughout the country people looked forward to their comedies; fans stood in line in rain and snow for the opportunity of laughing at what Arthur Knight calls "ordered insanity."

The term "slapstick" had its origin in an implement, used by stage comedians ages ago, made up of two flat pieces of wood which slapped together loudly when they hit an object, like someone's protruding posterior.

A British critic once defined slapstick as "an expression of laughter entirely free from literary contamination." The dictionary defines it as "crude comedy whose humor depends upon violent activity, horseplay, etc."

34

Sennett did more than anyone to update ancient techniques of slapstick, to adapt laugh-making techniques to the motion picture. Improvising as he went, he produced an average of two short films a week for many years.

"All Keystone comedians dealt in burlesque," said Sennett. "We made fun of a number of things, including burlesque itself."

There was scarcely a comedy made during the early days of the silent film that did not include a chase sequence.

The early comic approach to motion pictures was primarily visual. Sennett, particularly, had little time for intellectual considerations. Words were a nuisance to him. Action was his means of expression, and fast action, too. Thinking merely served to slow down the pace. So great, it is said, was his distrust for the written word that he forbade written scripts in his studio. Only late in his career did he permit any writing at all to take place.

According to the Sennett method, the director and the comedians created the picture as they went along. "The very texture of Mack Sennett films is visual," says an analysis issued by the Museum of Modern Art. "Profoundly ridiculous and flawlessly timed, the action develops spontaneously as in a dream, and is as universally comprehensible as a blow."

36

Sennett felt that the motion picture was a medium capable of being understood by everyone. Therefore, he was impatient from the start with anything that stood in the way of his elemental appeal to humor.

The crude eloquence of silent slapstick won a huge following throughout the nation where motion pictures were growing increasingly popular.

Often the germ of a picture would be a single gag. Two gags provided enough material to build a one-reel picture.

Gilbert Seldes, critic of the performing arts, says, "Keystone Comedies created an atmosphere of lunatic fantasy." James Agee, the critic, describes them as "just a shade faster and fuzzier than life." But perhaps the most characteristic tendency of the early comedies was irreverence for those in authority. In Keystone films, people in high places are never safe from attack, by land, by sea or by air.

Comedians had to be acrobats, had to know how to take falls and punishment. Perhaps this was a carry-over from the early circus clown and the burlesque funnymen.

Satire was part of the laugh-making arsenal, as was pantomime, and the various physical gestures that silent film demanded and comedy traditionally utilized. "The tyrannies of smug dignity," wrote Gene Fowler, "fell beneath Sennett's slapstick blows."

Hal Roach, who was Sennett's closest competition, specialized in a more cohesive type of comedy. There was less meaningless violence, and more of a blend of slapstick with other comedy techniques.

Roach had tremendous comic imagination and was a great discoverer of talent. For example, Roach had the imagination to picture the team of Laurel and Hardy and gave them every encouragement until they developed into the super-attraction that they did. He conceived the use of children and animals as featured comic players. His *Our Gang* comedies started in 1921 and became a national institution. Performers, such as Lloyd, testify that Roach was a good man to work for. He let them alone and permitted them elbow room to develop their special comic techniques.

In contrast, Sennett tended to try to dominate his performers and personally decided what was funny and what was not.

Whether on the Sennett or Roach lot, these staple tactics and techniques were used in building a comedy: speeding up action by cranking the camera slowly; the use of cloth brick and the break-away bottle and vase; the pursuit or chase; and always the prat fall.

Al St. John was one of the most popular comedians of his era.

Most early comedy sequences were unwritten, unplanned, and un- rehearsed. Left, Roscoe (Fatty) Arbuckle and Mabel Normand.

39

The central character in almost all early comedy situations was the policeman. He was not an ordinary law-enforcement officer. The comic policeman was a product of fantasy, a uniformed sprite who reduced authority to an absurdity. Obviously Mack Sennett had a strong interest in policemen. It is said that he once considered joining the force himself. It is not easy to analyze why his policemen seemed so funny. Perhaps most people have been victims of officiousness and welcome retribution, if only on the screen.

"Policemen are the most interesting thing on the screen," Mack Sennett once said. "When I get going, I'll have more policemen than Scotland Yard."

Mack Sennett's favorite cop was Ford Sterling, a former circus clown who had been an entertainer from his early childhood. He was a large, strong man, well suited to the rough-and-tumble slapstick comedy. Sterling was the most popular comedian of his day, and actually looked like a chief of police. The original Keystone policemen included Billy Hauber, Billy Gilbert, Slim Summerville, Bobby Dunn, Charles Avery, and Charlie Parrott, also known as Charlie Chase.

In early comedies, many actors had their start, at one time or another, as policemen.

Violence—pure mayhem—was an important feature of all early comedies. From star to extra, everyone had to know how to take falls, dangle from ropes, climb to high places, bounce back from blows on the head; and generally be as much an acrobat as an actor.

"I guess I've been bathed in no less than ten tons of very wet cement," commented Snub Pollard, popular comedian under Hal Roach. "I figured up once I have caught about fourteen thousand pies in my puss, and have been hit by over six hundred automobiles and two trains. Once I was even kicked by a giraffe."

Buster Keaton, one of the great comedians, comments: "Many cops knew nothing whatever about falling. No one had told them that *both* ends of the spine had to be protected when taking a fall. Or that for one kind of fall, you must relax your whole body, for another, you tighten up the muscles of both your back and backside. Although I have been called an acrobat," continues Keaton, "I would say I am only a half acrobat at the most. I did learn to fall as a kid, just as Chaplin, Lloyd, and (Douglas) Fairbanks did."

41

Mabel Normand, the impish comedian, some believe was the funniest female movie star of them all, is credited with throwing the first custard pie in a motion picture. The target was Ben Turpin, a cross-eyed comedian who had few equals when it came to taking a violent fall without doing himself permanent damage.

It appears that the cameras were grinding and Turpin was trying to be funny. Somehow, his crossed eyes were not sufficient to carry the scene. It wasn't comical. Unexpectedly something happened which not only rescued the movie from the doldrums but also made film history.

Mabel Normand was sitting quietly watching. She noticed Turpin's plight. She also noticed a custard pie on a bench nearby, part of the lunch of two stage carpenters.

Thousand of pies were thrown in the Hal Roach movie *The Battle of the Century* as Laurel and Hardy satirized motion picture slapstick of the day.

Never one to think first when a possible laugh was involved, Mabel picked up the pie, took aim, and let it go. It exploded without warning against its target. From a mass of dripping goo emerged two crossed eyes. Everyone roared with laughter while the camera kept grinding. "No one expected this memorable heave, least of all Turpin," recalled Sennett. "We seized upon pie-throwing after that, refined it, perfected its techniques, and presented it to the theater as a new art. It became, in time, a learned routine like the prat fall, the double-take, the slowburn, and the frantic leap, all stock equipment of competent comedians."

Edgar Kennedy in the act of pitching a pie.

A certain, albeit vague, motivation was demanded. While most comedies were highly improbable, they stayed within shooting distance of the possible. Certain locations were favorites because of their limitless comic potential. These included kitchens, hotel lobbies, beauty parlors, and barber shops. So frequently did these spots appear in early comedies that they were finally built permanently on the set.

Comedians even thought up a way to hurl pies around objects like telegraph poles. They accomplished this by the use of an expert fly-caster, who was beyond camera range, usually on a ladder. He could make a pie curve in any direction and still hit its target. One of the most popular and talented comedians, Fatty Arbuckle, "had the control of a major league pitcher," says Gene Fowler.

44

Force and violence were part of the everyday life of the early silent comedies. Syd Chaplin (Charlie's half brother) in *The Wild Waiter*.

Mack Sennett found that un-
draped young ladies won more
headlines for his motion pictures than comedians. Many
future stars began their careers
in Mack Sennett bathing suits,
such as Phyllis Haver *(right)*.

One day, Mack Sennett—so the story goes—came to the conclusion that cops and comedians were all right, but it took
pretty girls in scant costumes to get front-page publicity. "I'm
going to collect some of the prettiest girls for bathing-beauty
comedies," he announced.

He did. Los Angeles and Hollywood were attracting fair
maidens from all over the nation, who had come to filmland
to become motion picture stars. Most of them had difficulty
getting before a camera for even the most minor assignment.
Sennett supplied a valuable entrance to motion picture work for
such glamorous ladies. All they needed was a bathing suit
and willingness, on occasion, to get in the way of a flying custard pie.

This was the era, too, of the speeded-up film. Since the early
cameras were turned by hand, turning the crank slowly in-
creased the speed of the picture. Turning fast resulted in slow
motion. Thus, the camera man had control over what the speed
of the picture actually would be. In some instances, where
the camera man wanted to save film, he would crank slowly,
and the picture would whizz by the audience with superhuman speed.

47

Hal Roach's *Our Gang* with a visitor—the poet Carl Sandburg.

Charlie Chase, comedian who made a "straight" role a laugh-maker.

"The making of the Keystone comedy was a free-wheeling enterprise," stated Adolph Zukor, famous movie producer. "Everybody from Sennett down took a hand. Directors and players were allowed to improvise almost at will, so long as additional expense was not involved." Spontaneity and a feeling that anything was possible as long as it was funny, permitted early comedies a flexibility unknown in today's entertainment world.

Spontaneity was perhaps the most characteristic feature of the era. Clarence Badger, a veteran of the early days of motion picture, points out: "The stories for Keystone comedies as constructed by Sennett writers never existed on paper. They were simply 'fished for' created by being built up bit by bit, and carried in the writers' heads. The director assigned always took part in the story conferences. It was up to him to memorize the story, the gags and the situations agreed upon.

49

"Incidentally, a session of Keystone writers in the heat of a palaver, expressing their ideas with rhapsodical antics, explosive and salty explanations, was likened to a gathering of badly deranged lunatics."

Another old-timer recollects that "a gag conference consisted of about six gag men and Mack Sennett. There was no orderly procedure. The story was attacked from all angles by everybody. Anyone who thought up a funny situation would not only tell it, but act it out at the same time. One gag would suggest another, and often two joke smiths would combine their gags into one routine."

In discussing his experience with Mack Sennett, Bing Crosby says: "Those shorts had a running time of about twenty minutes. Sennett didn't shoot scenes over and over again. Once was enough. With a two-day shooting schedule, he couldn't waste time. At the end, we wound up with a chase. I'd get into a car with a girl and would start out over the Hollywood hills with the cops or the irate parent in pursuit, while Sennett had his camera men crank slowly to make it look fast."

With all their shortcomings, the repetitious, obvious, jerky, ill-planned Sennett and Roach comedies were supreme in the comedy world as long as the one- and two-reel comedy was a national favorite. When the motion picture managers began to move in the direction of double-feature bills, one- and two-reel comedies were doomed. The spot occupied by Sennett, Roach, and Christie was taken over by a featured star, such as Charlie Chaplin, Buster Keaton, or Harold Lloyd.

Performers in Keystone comedies included some of the most famous names in show business: Louise Fazenda, Gloria Swanson, Roscoe Arbuckle, Polly Moran, Chester Conklin, Ford Sterling, Mack Swain, Phyllis Haver, Harold Lloyd, Charlie Murray, Andy Clyde, Carole Lombard, Clyde Cook, Hank Mann, Marie Prevost, W. C. Fields, Wallace Beery, Marie Dressler, Bing Crosby, and many more.

Ben Turpin might have tried to curl his hair, but he never thought of straightening his eyes, which were worth big money to him and the Keystone Film Company.

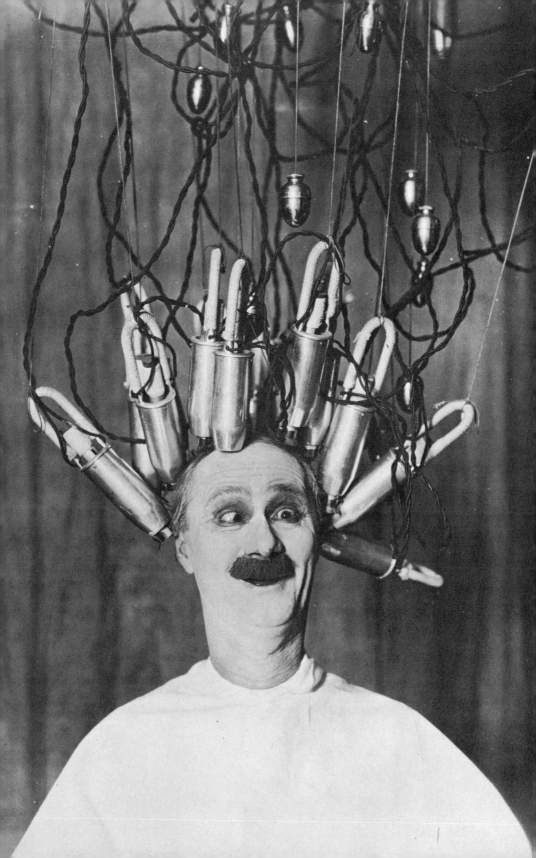

Hal Roach productions brought forward such favorites of the day as Charlie Chase, Snub Pollard, Bebe Daniels, Ruth Roland, Stan Laurel, Oliver Hardy, *Our Gang* juveniles, Jackie Cooper, Patsy Kelly, Thelma Todd, Matt Moore, Lillian Rich, Will Rogers, and many more including, of course, Harold Lloyd.

"Keystone comedies are predicaments," said Gilbert Seldes, "life's little ironies translated into grotesques and projected in the ceaseless flow of movement. The population of the Keystone world consists of scamps, scoundrels, shysters, fakers, tramps—outcasts, in short order—with policemen and pretty girls as foils to their activities. A little later, the poor and oppressed, the waiters and barbers and show girls, appear; but the successful, well-groomed, alert, and smart American never appears."

From such beginnings, came full-length films which delighted audiences around the world. And the alert, well-groomed American did eventually appear in the person of a young man with pancake make-up and eyeglasses whose name was Harold Lloyd.

Hal Roach, pioneer comedy producer who helped make film history *(left);* the camera man *(right)* never knew from moment to moment what risks he was to undergo.

Harold Lloyd, Charlie Chaplin,
and Douglas Fairbanks.

CHAPTER THREE

The Funny Men

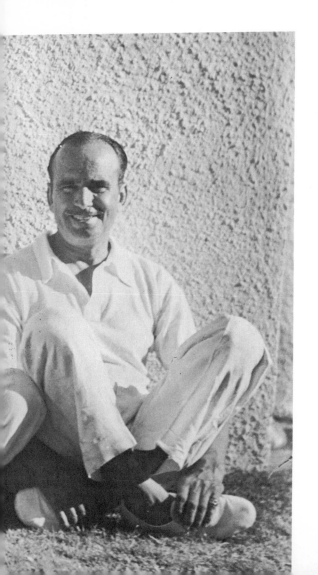

There have not always been stars in the film firmament. In the early days, the show was the thing; and motion pictures were made with more or less anonymous players.

One Keystone director reported working on a motion picture without knowing the cast personnel.

"How about the cast?" he inquired of Sennett.

"Don't worry," Sennett replied. "It doesn't matter a damn who's in it."

One way of avoiding emphasis on personalities, as the public increasingly grew star conscious, was simply to announce, "All Star Cast."

But, although film companies feared that star-making would send salaries booming, the rise of the star system was inevitable. In fact, as the movie industry became part of the big-business life of the nation, producers began voluntarily to build personalities. They had discovered that the public rushed in greater numbers to see a star. The presence of a popular actor or actress literally guaranteed a movie's success.

Florence Lawrence was one of the first dramatic stars of motion pictures. Flora Finch was another, and Mary Pickford followed. The list grew. Inevitably the star system reached into the world of comedy which Mack Sennett commanded. In this world, the earliest American personality featured was John Bunny, followed by Ford Sterling. Max Linder, the French comedian, was a pioneer comedy star and exerted strong influence on the course of American film fun.

The super-star emerging on the comedy scene was an artist whose name became almost synonymous with comedy itself— Charles Chaplin.

As a pantomimist, Charles Chaplin had no equal in motion pictures. *(Right)* Chaplin with the famous motion picture comedienne Mabel Normand.

"Charlie was one of the world's great pantomime comedians," says Harold Lloyd. "He had a tremendous background of training in the English music halls and an innate knowledge of comedy. This gave him a natural bent for timing and spacing.

"It was this timing and spacing that was so difficult for me to learn in my early days of comedy. I recall very vividly how I was told by John Lane Connor to get the most out of laughs and not to talk over them. This ability to time and space your gags and jokes is so important that many comedians are able to get by with mediocre jokes if their timing and spacing sensitivity is developed.

"Charlie Chaplin had this sensitivity to an extreme. Like all great comedians, he had an instinct for what was right and just how far he could go. He worked on the borderline between

comedy and tragedy. Some of his themes could easily have been dramas, but he pushed them over to the side of comedy.

"The appeal of his little tramp, the feeling for the down-trodden man, fit into a lot of other people's lives and gained him immense sympathy. Charlie also developed many mannerisms that helped make the character popular—the little walk, the tricks with the cane and the derby, his way of going around corners. These things were not only clever and comical, but ingenious in their conception. He had a fine sense of comedy and surrounded himself with good gag men."

For Lloyd, physical comedy, the visual gag, was an important element. "Most successful comedians are funny not only in their facial expressions, but the way their bodies express themselves," says Lloyd. "One of the reasons television is handicapped when it comes to comedy is that you're too close up.

But comedians in the early days didn't have to be close up. The way they moved their feet, their arms, their shoulders, the way they stood, or fell, were all funny.

"Chaplin worked tremendously hard on his pictures. He had all the requirements necessary to win the acclaim and the popularity that he got. There are many different situations that comedians encounter which help make them popular or endear them to the public," says Lloyd. "A comedian has to gain more than just a laughing action. The audience must laugh *with* him. The comedian that just has you laugh *at* him very seldom becomes a great comedian. The audience has to root for him. The audience has to sympathize with him. The audience must work for him. Of course, the comedian has to be funny, too.

"There is such a thing as competition between some comedians and the audience. With Chaplin, the audience never felt this competition arising. The audience was clearly superior to him.

"Of course, Chaplin's gags had to be good, like any other comedian's. You simply can't rise above your material. But, give the same material to ten different comedians, and they all may be great at it. Magnificent. But each has his own conception; each has his own way of doing it. Some comedians like to take inconsequential material and build on it. Others take material that is funny in itself and time it and space it beautifully. They get the maximum laughs out of it that way."

Chaplin was Mack Sennett's big find. He first thought that Chaplin could be funny as an imitation of Ford Sterling, wearing long mustaches and a frock coat. But Chaplin wanted to evolve a character of his own, which he created by borrowing baggy pants, big shoes, and an ill-fitting coat from actors on the lot who were much bigger than he.

"Costumes like Chaplin's had been worn by other comedians in England," says Lloyd; "not exactly the way Charlie wore it but, in general, something like it. The costume was absolutely ideal for Charlie because he became a different type of tramp. It was sufficiently off beat to permit him to become the best pantomimist, I believe, that the world has ever known."

Chaplin's technique of comedy proved fundamentally different from that of Mack Sennett. The action of Sennett comedies was fast, decisive. There was no time to build up to a gag. Chaplin, on the contrary, was accustomed to a more leisurely pace. He was hardly able to get started before Sennett expected him to be finished and on to another laugh situation.

It was generally recognized on the Sennett lot that the boss expected a gag to be started and finished in approximately twenty feet of film. Chaplin took more than one hundred feet before he even got going. But Chaplin's inability to conform to Sennett slapstick techniques was to contribute to a new school of film comedy, raising slapstick to the status of an art.

Chaplin's humor had an amazing effect on almost all the comedians of his era, and after. For many years, there was scarcely a comedian in the United States, and in many other parts of the world, who could operate without showing some of the influences of the Chaplin walk, the Chaplin clothes, the Chaplin smile, the Chaplin way of winning laughs. Such was the Chaplin genius.

Of course, Chaplin had his teachers. They included Max Linder, Mack Sennett, and Mabel Normand, Sennett's famous leading lady and chief comedienne. According to Sennett, "Mabel Normand and Charlie Chaplin had much in common. She was as deft at pantomime as he. She worked in slapstick, but her stage business and her gestures were subtle, not broad." A former model, Mabel Normand became one of the most popular film actresses of her era. "Mabel Normand could do everything that Chaplin could do," said Sennett. "To me, she was the greatest comedienne that ever lived." It was seeing Mabel Normand in a bathing suit that gave Sennett his first idea for bathing beauties in his films.

"Mabel Normand is a creature of impulse," said Sam Goldwyn, the famous motion picture producer. "She never calculates a moment ahead for fear that the moment itself might calculate something she likes better. When she works, she works hard, but she can't do it in step with the hour hand."

This spontaneity fit well in the comedy films of the Sennett period. "It is the presence of Mabel Normand in the cast which saves it from being just another of those things," wrote Robert E. Sherwood. "You can't imagine this irrepressive gamin doing anything stupid or dull or obvious on the screen. She has a remarkable flair for impudent comedy. . . ."

Mabel was incapable of assuming a dignity that she didn't think she had. She was a practical joker and a mimic. This was ideal equipment for early comedy films. She knew little fear. She would jump from high cliffs, dive into the water, ride dangerous horses. According to one source, she jumped no less than twenty-two times from a boat deck into a rough sea until the episode being photographed was deemed satisfactory. Often she went home exhausted and ill. A doctor once told her she must be more careful of her safety and health. Her answer: "What in hell is the difference if it makes a lot of people laugh?"

According to Gene Fowler, a story called for Mabel to be dragged by a horse through the mud. "After she had washed up and put on clean clothes, she was interviewed by a lady who asked, 'I suppose the hardships of motion picture actresses are overestimated?'

"Mabel was too tired to explain. 'Yes,' she said. 'It is an exceedingly monotonous life.'"

Another great comic spirit of the era was Buster Keaton, whose silent comedies are among the masterpieces of American films. "In actuality, Keaton was Chaplin's equal in inventiveness, his superior in sheer acrobatic grace," says Christopher Bishop in *Film Quarterly*. "Instead of Chaplin's pathos, which is coming to seem a little uncomfortable and maudlin as the years pass, Keaton presented a cool, pure and absolutely unsentimental comic vision."

"I was always puzzled later on when people spoke of similarities in the characters Charlie Chaplin and I played in the movies," says Keaton in *My Wonderful World of Slapstick*. "There was, to me, a basic difference from the start. Charlie's tramp was a bum with the bum's philosophy. Lovable as he was, he would steal if he got the chance. My little fellow was a working man and honest . . . Harold Lloyd's screen character was quite different from both Chaplin's and mine. He played a Momma's boy who continually surprised everyone, including himself, by triumphing over an impossible situation and displaying, in fits and starts, the fighting heart of a lion."

"Buster had a tremendous training," says Lloyd. "As a little boy, he was in vaudeville with his parents. There was a trio, and, as I recall, he dressed like his father. His father appeared to treat him terribly, threw him all around. Buster learned the knack of making falls better than any other comic I know.

"He could make the funniest falls and the most weird ones, and he knew how to do it without getting hurt. But underneath that, Buster was a true comedian. He learned the art of timing and spacing, which is basic to all comics. Buster created a character that was comic to look at, in the little way he walked, the clothes that he wore, and, of course, his characteristic of never smiling. By not smiling, Buster made his task all the more difficult. Like all good comics his body movements were generally funny. But he had to depend on his body and go along on that same facial expression."

Buster Keaton's film *The General* was one of the masterpieces of the silent-film era.

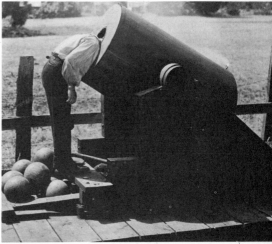

63

Harold Lloyd considered Keaton one of half a dozen great film comedians. "Chaplin didn't handicap himself like Buster did," says Lloyd. "Chaplin could smile or do anything he wanted, which helped him tremendously. He could not have been the great pantomimist that he was if he had to keep a stony face like Buster.

"Buster knew gags. He knew how to put them together and to condition them. And his conception of his character and the way he did it was excellent. That's what a comedian has to do. He has to know his own character thoroughly. He has to know comedy, at least the type of comedy that he's doing. Every comedian has to be a scholar in comedy so that he can know just what he is doing."

Keaton was once asked why he never smiled. "I just work that way because I learned as a kid growing up, with an audience, that I just had to be that type of comedian. Fans early taught me another thing about my work I had not known. A few fan letters asked why the little man in these pictures never smiled. We had been unaware of it. We looked at three two-reelers we had done together and found it to be true. Later, just for fun, I tried smiling at the end of one picture. The preview audience hated it and hooted the scene. After that, I never smiled again on stage, screen or television."

"There is no question but that Harold Lloyd was one of the great contributors to the comedy of motion pictures," says Keaton. "His was the inventive knack of situations; no one could ever forget his antics with the big clock in *Safety Last*. He was indeed a product of the movies. While Charlie Chaplin and I came from the stage, Harold used the camera for tricky effects with consummate skill."

Buster Keaton's comic pantomime was doubly difficult because his facial expression never changed.

"All sorts of laurels have been handed to slapstick comedies that Chaplin, Lloyd, Harry Langdon, and I made," says Keaton. "They have been acclaimed as screen classics, as masterpieces of the comic art. This is most flattering, but it came as a complete surprise to me. I never realized I was doing anything but trying to make people laugh when I threw my custard pies and took prat falls."

Harry Langdon was another great comedian of this era. "I originally saw him doing an act called *Johnny's New Car*," says Harold Lloyd, "and I told Hal Roach that he would make a good comic for films. Hal went down to the Orpheum in Los Angeles and saw Harry. And he agreed. But they had a difference of opinion—about one hundred dollars worth, and Harry went with another producer and then landed with Sennett.

"After a few pictures, Harry came to me and said, 'Harold, I don't seem to be scoring.' I had seen his comedies and I thought I knew why.

"'They're working you too fast,' I told him. 'They have a habit of doing that at Sennett; they did the same to Chaplin. Slow down, and make them play to you, the way Charlie does; don't play to them.'

"Harry slowed down, and he was much better. But he slowed down a little too much, and finally I told him one day, 'Harry I didn't mean for you to drag it.'

"Harry was called the baby-face comedian," says Lloyd. "It was an apt description, for his actions were like that of a little boy. He'd start to do something, then he'd change. Indecision was an integral part of his character. Also innocence.

"He was a fine pantomimist and had all the essentials of success. Unfortunately, he lacked the judgment to decide what he should or shouldn't do. Later on, he became his own boss, and, like many in our business, he was more fit to be the comic than to act as the guiding light. He could have been infinitely greater had he allowed someone else to direct his career."

Harry Langdon

Harry Langdon brought a special naivete to silent comedy films.

Harry had a kind of "dough-faced, baby innocence about him combined with malice," said Sennett. "Like Chaplin, you had to let him take his time and go through his motions. His twitters and hesitations built up a ridiculous but sympathetic little character. It was difficult for us at first to know how to use Langdon, accustomed as we were to firing the gags and the falls as fast as possible. But as new talent arrived we found ways to screen it and to cope with it. I thought for a while Langdon was as good as Chaplin, and in some of his pathetic scenes, he was certainly as good."

Harold Lloyd considers Langdon innately a funny man, and one of our great comics. "The other comedians I would rate as tops in this era were the team of Laurel and Hardy," says Lloyd. "This team started together in silent comedies and reached their greatest success in the talkies. As Chaplin was Sennett's greatest discovery, Laurel and Hardy were the greatest find of Hal Roach.

"Laurel came to Roach at the time when I was still associated with him. Later he teamed up with Hardy, and they formed a perfect complement. A product of the English music halls, from which Chaplin had come, Laurel was close to Charlie in his field of pantomime. He was a great comedian. Hardy was a fine comedian, too.

"Their appeal was that of a couple of struggling characters, kind of in-between tramps and working men. They were always buddies, but always had differences that would get them into trouble. One reacted differently from the other in the same situation.

Oliver Hardy and Stan Laurel before they formed a team.

"They developed many characteristics—the slow burn of Hardy's, the cry that Laurel had, and the constant bickering. They also worked the borderline between comedy and tragedy, but usually on the broader side. They were probably the best team we ever had in comedies."

Both Laurel and Hardy had been in the movies for many years before they came together and jelled as a team. Laurel had already been in the movies as a comedian. He came to America from England as an understudy to Chaplin in the Karno Pantomime Company. Oliver Hardy began his moving picture career with Mack Sennett and specialized in being a comedy "heavy."

Laurel's character was that of an innocent, very trusting individual. Hardy, his partner, had a greater sophistication and a sort of flowery approach to things which contrasted with the naïveté of his partner.

Stan Laurel, the mentor of the team, believed that true comedy cannot possibly depend upon the spoken word, despite the fact that the team was a success in the talkies. "Comics now lean too much on the line gag and not the visual gag," he says. "I think that Hollywood comics, these days, are talking too much and not doing enough." According to Professor John McCabe, in his book *Mr. Laurel and Mr. Hardy*, a friend once approached Laurel and asked what comedy was. "That floored me," said Laurel. "What is comedy? I don't know. Does anybody? Can you define it? I learned how to get laughs, and that's all I know about it. You have to learn what people will laugh at, and then proceed accordingly. First of all, you should start out with a fairly believable plot, no matter how broad it is, and then work on from there.

Many performers owe much to the team of Laurel and Hardy. For example, the famous stare of Oliver Hardy has been carried over by such comedians as Jack Benny and Johnny Carson, while Dick Van Dyke owes a debt to Stan Laurel.

Laurel and Hardy slapstick short films become a popular favorite
with motion picture viewers almost all over the world.

"But you've got to *learn* how to get on from there. Nobody's
going to teach you. That's why one of the best ways for a young
comedian to learn his trade is to do as much summer stock work
as possible. Appearing in repertoire, changing parts, being in
different situations over and over again, all help him learn the
'feel' of different audiences.

"He has to learn why certain gags go over and why they don't. You develop an intuition after facing various types of audiences. What one will laugh at, another won't and vice versa. One day you will know; then you're in business."

"Roach was most instrumental in bringing Laurel into motion pictures," says Lloyd. "He worked for Roach singly at first, and Laurel came about as close as any of the comedians I can think of to what Charlie Chaplin did in certain types of pantomime. When he teamed up with Hardy, there was a complete rapport.

"If I had to choose between the two, I would immediately pick Laurel, because I feel he could have become great alone, and I don't think Hardy could have. That isn't belittling Hardy, because in the team, Hardy was as good as Laurel; he was a perfect balance and a counterpoint to throw back. You have to judge them as a team, the way they have become famous and loved. When they put Laurel and Hardy on television, the team became just as popular as it was originally, showing that basically comedy doesn't change."

These, then, were some of the great comedians of the silent days. But there was another comedian of equal stature whose popularity was vast and whose contributions to the technique of comedy were considerable. He was, of course, Harold Lloyd himself.

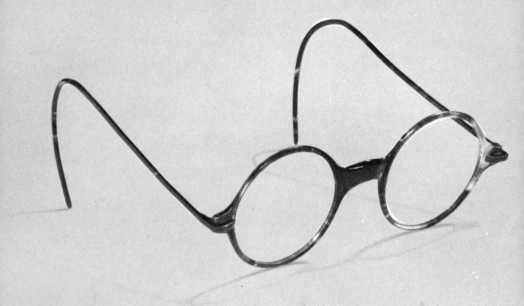

CHAPTER FOUR

Who Ever Heard of a Comedian With Glasses?

"You'll never get anywhere in comedy," Ford Sterling had told Harold Lloyd early in his career. "But I think you can act. Why don't you go see D. W. Griffith?"

But circumstances were not to permit the young Lloyd, interested as he was in drama, to take the advice seriously. In the year 1915 Hal Roach was a husky young extra seeking a career in the movies. When he inherited a little money, Roach decided to set himself up in the business of making films, especially comedies.

The original Harold Lloyd glasses.

Harold Lloyd's first successful comedy character was called Lonesome Luke.

But Roach did not find it easy to locate a talented comedian. He hired a British comic but was not impressed with his work.

One day Roach approached Lloyd with a proposition. "Why not try your hand at comedy?" he suggested. "I think you can do a lot better than the man I have now. You be my new comedian."

Harold agreed. The salary was set at five dollars a day.

"Think up some funny get-up and let's get going," said Roach.

"I experimented with dress and make-up and settled on a character we christened 'Willie Work,' Lloyd recalls. "The name wrongly suggested a tramp. It was, instead, a hash of different low comedy get-ups, with heavily padded coat shoulders, a battered silk hat, and a cat's whiskers mustache as its distinguishing marks.

"In one Willie Work picture, Roach thought up the droll idea of putting me in bed with a skunk. The pole cat's first line of defense had been removed and Roach told me that he had read somewhere that a skunk so treated makes a perfect pet, and is playful as a kitten. Evidently the skunk misunderstood, because he bit me.

"A program was mapped out calling for a one-reel comedy one week and a two-reel drama the next. In the comedies, I was to have the lead. But when I discovered that another actor, the dramatic lead, was getting ten dollars a day and I only five dollars, I demanded equal pay. Roach refused. Thereupon, I left the Roach organization and was hired by Mack Sennett Productions.

"My experience with Keystone comedies was mostly a series of falls, and I soon learned how to make them without breaking my neck. My big test on the Sennett lot was whether I could fall or whether I was just another upright actor."

Working for Sennett involved churning out picture after picture, sometimes finishing a film in three days. Lloyd was fast learning to keep pace with Keystone productions when he was asked to return to work with the Hal Roach Company at fifty dollars a week. It was a raise not to be refused.

The first question Roach asked him upon his return was, "How about a new character?"

This was the period when Chaplin was at the height of his popularity. His success with funny clothes and his mannerisms were being imitated not only by amateurs throughout the country but by professionals as well. Motion picture exhibitors who could not get the original Chaplin films were seeking imitations. So great was Chaplin's influence that anyone who did not ape him was not a comedian!

"I told Roach that I thought I had an improvement on the Willie Work character," says Lloyd. "My father helped me design a new costume. He found a worn pair of size 12-AA shoes in a repair shop in Los Angeles. He added a black-and-white vertically striped shirt and discovered a coat at a women's tailor shop and a pair of very tight short trousers, as well as a vest that

was much too short, a cut-down collar, and a cut-down hat. This costume, together with two dots for a mustache completed the costume for my new character who was named Lonesome Luke.

"The cunning thought behind all this was to reverse the Chaplin outfit. All his clothes were too large. Mine were going to be too small. My shoes were funny but different. My mustache was funny but different, as well. Despite the fact that my costume was a direct reversal of Chaplin's, it was purely imitative."

But the country was hungry for comedy. Harold's new character became immensely popular throughout the United States and even abroad.

"The picture always ended with two hundred feet of chase.

Harold Lloyd with Hal Roach *(left)*. Will Rogers was to write of them years later: "Twenty years of furnishing the entire world with laughs is not a bad epitaph on anybody's tombstone." *(Right)* Harold with his father.

There was something akin to college spirit in the comedy film companies of the early silent pictures. *Center,* Harold Lloyd as Lonesome Luke, surrounded by actors and technicians. Immediately behind Harold Lloyd is Hal Roach and in front, Bebe Daniels.

I was pursued by dogs, sheriffs, angry housewives, circus tigers, motor cars, baby carriages, wild bulls, trolley cars, locomotives, and of course, legions of cops.

"During those days, there was no such thing as a written scenario. A camera man, a girl, and a comedian would start off down the road, with Hal Roach directing. Usually we had no particular idea in mind. We would just look for an incident that might set the comic wheels turning. Usually we found one. We would improvise on the moment, and together with prat falls, chases, and the throwing of articles of one kind or another, some sort of a comedy would emerge."

Starting in January, 1916, Lloyd made nearly one hundred Lonesome Luke one-reel films. They were made for the Rolin Company and distributed by Pathe. Production carried on at the rate of one or two and sometimes even three pictures a week.

On April 10, 1917, the *New York Mirror* commented, "To have become in less than eighteen months a comedian so popular as to be ranked with the leaders in that line, and one who is an advertised attraction in many theaters, is the story of Harold Lloyd's achievements in the Pathe Lonesome Luke comedies."

"Screen comedy," the *Mirror* went on, "especially of the rough-and-tumble sort, demands unusual athletic ability. Mr. Lloyd possesses this to a marked degree, being an excellent rider, swimmer, fencer, and boxer. He also excels as a tumbler, and it is this accomplishment which enables him to do stunts in his comedies which do not seem humanly possible."

But though the Lonesome Luke character was popular, Harold Lloyd never liked it. It was rigid and gave very little leeway for development. It was something of an imitation, but other comedians were doing the same thing; it almost seemed to be necessary.

But Charlie Chaplin was king of the type of comedy that Lonesome Luke represented. And Harold Lloyd saw no future in trying to squeeze Chaplin from his throne.

"I was looking for something individual," says Lloyd. "I was looking for a character who would be my own. I would rather have been a serious actor than continue as an imitation.

81

exclusi[...]
[...] hereof, and
[...] [...] [...] [...] [...] upon the following
terms and c[...]itions:

1. Lloyd shall faithfully, and to the best of his ability, play
any parts in the production of any or all films produced by Rolin during
the continuance of this agreement, at such times and places as Rolin
shall, from time to time, direct.

2. Lloyd shall receive, and hereby agrees to accept, and Rolin
agrees to pay to Lloyd, in full for all services to be rendered by Lloyd
hereunder, the sum of Fifty Dollars per week, commencing Monday February
7, 1916, payable to Lloyd at the end of each week of service hereunder.

3. Lloyd further agrees to and with Rolin that Rolin shall have
the right to renew this agreement, and Lloyd agrees to accept and comply
with said renewal, at the end of said six months period, upon the same
terms and conditions, except that Lloyd's compensation for service during
said second six months period shall be One Hundred Dollars per week.

4. In consideration of aforesaid employment, Lloyd further gives
and grants to Rolin the right to renew this agreement, for a further
and succeeding period of one year, at end of second six months period,
on like terms and conditions, except that Lloyd's compensation for
service during said yearly period shall be One Hundred Fifty Dollars
per week.

5. In consideration of aforesaid employment, Lloyd further gives
and grants to Rolin the right to renew this agreement for a further
and succeeding period of one year, at end of yearly period last above
mentioned, on like terms and conditions, except that Lloyd's compensation
for service during said yearly period shall be Three Hundred Dollars
per week.

6. In consideration of aforesaid employment and of the advertising
and publicity which Lloyd will receive in his profession through the
release of these films, Lloyd promises and agrees to and with Rolin
that he will not, during the continuance of this agreement, or any re-
newals or options which Rolin shall exercise hereunder, appear or take
part in any film or legitimate production, except those produced by Rolin

7. Rolin shall have the right to terminate this agreement at any
time during any of the periods hereunder, in the event said contract
with Pathe Exchange, Inc., is terminated, or in the event of other
occurrences, or Act of God, or man, beyond Rolin's control.

8. This agreement supersedes and supplants all former agreements.

In Witness Whereof, Rolin has caused this instrument to be duly
executed, and its corporate seal thereunto affixed, by its officers
duly thereunto authorized, and said Lloyd has hereunto set his hand and
seal, on the day and year and at the place first above written.

Executed and delivered
in presence of

W. H. Doane

ROLIN FILM COMPANY

By *H E Roach* President

By _____ Secretary

× *H E Lloyd*

The contract that lured Harold Lloyd away from Mack Sennett
and back to Hal Roach in 1916. Note point 2, which stipulates
that Lloyd is to be paid fifty dollars a week for his services.

"I wanted to be a fellow who wouldn't be ridiculous on the screen if the story of a boy-and-girl romance came along. I wanted to wear decent, or at least appropriate, clothes.

"Then as now," recalls Harold, "it was thought an obvious advantage for a comedian to have an established character in a series of pictures instead of trying a new role with each new picture. In this way, the comedian is readily recognized as he first flashes on the screen."

With this in mind, Lloyd proposed to the Pathe Company, for whom he worked, that a new character be created. The company was not at all sympathetic.

"We have spent a great deal of money in making and advertising Lonesome Luke," they told him, "and who is Harold Lloyd anyway?"

"But I didn't want to go on forever being a third-rate imitator of anybody—even such a talented person as Chaplin," Lloyd remembers. "So I kept on the lookout for a new character, a character that would give me the flexibility and the originality that I basically needed."

In the back of Harold Lloyd's mind an idea was taking shape. "I had been thinking for a long time about a youth, possibly a boy, who could be carried through a series of college films, a comedy Frank Merriwell, when I saw a dramatic picture at a downtown theater. The central character in the movie was a fighting parson, tolerant and peaceful until riled, and then a tartar. Glasses emphasized a contrast between his appearance and what he actually was.

"The 'heavy' character in the movie had stolen the girl, carrying her away on horseback. The parson leaped on another horse, pursued and overtook the villain, dragged him from his horse, and the two were lost in a cloud of dust.

"When the dust cleared," Lloyd recalls, "the 'heavy' lay prone and still, while the parson dusted off his clothes with a careless flick of his handkerchief, replaced his glasses, and resumed his ministerial calm."

Harold did not feel cut out to be a fighting parson, but the basic idea appealed to him. He talked over his comedy idea with friends, and slowly the idea began to evolve. Glasses would serve as a trademark and at the same time suggest the character—quiet, normal, boyish, clean, sympathetic, not inconceivable in romance.

"I would need no eccentric make-up, no mustache or funny clothes. I would be an average, recognizable American youth and let the situation take care of the comedy. The comedy should be better for not depending upon a putty nose or its equivalent; the situation should be better for not being tied to low-comedy coat tails. Exaggeration is the breath of picture comedies, and while they cannot be true to life, they can be recognizably related to life.

"Probably the vision was not so clear in my mind at the time as all this," says Harold. "What I say now benefits by hindsight. Yet I saw it clearly enough.

"I was then getting one hundred dollars a week for long, hard work. It was a fortune in relation to my past earnings, but nothing compared to Charlie Chaplin's reported one thousand dollars a week salary. I again told Roach I was completely fed up with the Luke character. But I was convinced that Pathe would never agree to a change, and I resolved to go into dramatic pictures, where at least I could do something that was satisfying for me.

"However, Hal Roach was going to be in New York, and he promised to present the matter to the Pathe executives there. I was convinced that the company would refuse my suggestion and would hire some other comedian to take over the Lonesome Luke character.

"Hal Roach must have presented my case better than I anticipated because when he returned, he had the permission of the Pathe people for me to go ahead. The only question was whether to make one- or two-reel pictures with the new character.

"I decided to make one-reel pictures. One-reel subjects still were popular with exhibitors. We could make and release a program a week. A new character needed a constant hammering, I believed, in order for him to make a starting impression with the public.

"So, at the age of twenty-four, I was launched on my new

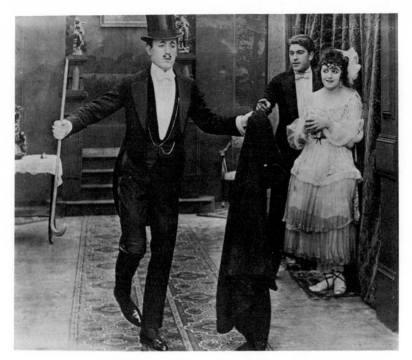

Harold Lloyd in a dressed-up version of Lonesome Luke.

character, which was indeed to be a sharp change from anything I had ever attempted before.

"I remember hunting through a tray containing probably
thirty pairs of glasses before coming upon the right one. The
first pair brought out of stock were too heavy. The second pair
were so large in diameter the rims went above my eyebrows
and killed a great deal of expression. The third pair just suited.
I wore them for a year and a half, guarding them with my life.
When the frame broke from wear and tear, I went on patching
it with everything from paste to spirit gum for three months,
until progressive dissolution forced us to send them east to an
optical-goods manufacturer for duplication.

"The manufacturer shipped us back twenty pairs tailored to
the measure of the old faithfuls and returned our check. The
advertising we had given tortoise-shell rims, they wrote, still
left them in our debt.

Harold sparked a craze for tortoise-shell glasses, from the cradle on up. *Right*, Harold Lloyd with his brother, Gaylord.

"Actually, it was mere chance that my glasses were horn-rimmed. The parson's glasses in the dramatic picture which inspired them were not tortoise shells, but when I came to choose a pair of my own, the vogue of horn rims was new, and many young people were wearing them. The novelty was a picture asset, and the suggestion of youth fitted perfectly with the character I had in mind.

"We took out the lenses immediately, knowing that the reflection of light on the glass would be troublesome.

"The first motion picture I made in my new character was entitled *Over the Fence,* which I wrote and directed myself."

The Glass Character, as Lloyd calls him, was introduced at a time when Hollywood was under sharp attack for its alleged indiscretions. Distaste and abhorrence for the film acting profession and its geographical center, Hollywood, was growing. If Hollywood was known as America's most glamorous city, it had also achieved an equally widespread reputation as a community for sensationalism. Newspapers found that screen personalities made interesting copy. Every deviation from the routine was made the subject of public scrutiny.

As a result of the notoriety, some children were actually forbidden by their elders to visit Hollywood. Mae Marsh, who was to become one of the famous actresses of the era, joined the caste of *The Birth of a Nation* when an undergraduate at Hollywood High School. As a result, she was snubbed by her friends and teachers. Her life was made so miserable because she worked in the movies that she was forced to leave school. When some of her fellow students visited the studio, they were expelled from school.

The moralistic teachings of *McGuffey's Readers* were reflected in Frank Merriwell adventures, Lady Bountiful cartoons, Horatio Alger, Jr. Books, and other writings of the early 1900's. Harold Lloyd exaggerated these teachings just enough to make them comical; but not enough to make them ridiculous. In Lloyd's world, virtue was usually rewarded; but in odd ways.

Young Lloyd in an early portrait, wearing his glasses and a flowing black tie, which he was later to discard.

It was against such a background that a new type of American hero was launched.

"My character was essentially a funny character, even though he looked like anyone else on the street. Like Chaplin, I represented a certain group. In my case it was yonng people working at a vocation and always struggling against the bigger guy."

The Glass Character was introduced in 1917. Three years later, Pathe announced it had signed Harold Lloyd to a contract "involving more than $1,500,000 during the first year." The deal, said the newspapers, "establishes Harold Lloyd as the highest-priced actor in the world."

The nation and the world grew to know Harold Lloyd almost as a member of the family through such one-reel films as *Take a Chance; Look Out Below; Here Come the Girls; Fireman, Save My Child.* Then came two-reel films such as *Bumping Into Broadway* and *From Hand to Mouth.* By 1920, there was *High and Dizzy* and *Number Please,* followed a year later by three-reel films, *Now or Never; Among Those Present;* and *Never Weaken.*

On August 24, 1919, when Harold was twenty-six, he was asked by the studio to pose for still pictures to be used in promoting his latest movie. Among the various props was a papier-maché bomb constructed for comedy use.

As the photographer was snapping pictures, Harold lit what was supposed to be a prop "bomb" and held it in a comic pose. Unfortunately, the "prop" turned out to be the real thing, accidentally placed among papier-mâché imitations. The bomb exploded. Harold was almost killed on the spot.

The explosion wrecked the building and injured several people around. Harold's hand was badly injured. His eyes and face were severely burned. For a time, it was feared he would lose his sight. He spent months in the hospital.

It was not until much later that he found his vision had been spared. His face healed with scarcely a scar.

Ten months after the accident, he was back at work, completing his picture *Haunted Spooks,* which he had been working on when the accident took place.

The only permanent damage was the injury to Lloyd's

right hand. It was a serious handicap. To be a great comedian requires the expressive participation of a performer's entire body—his eyes, his shoulders, his feet, the way he holds his head, the way he uses his hands. But Harold Lloyd now faced the fact that the use of one hand was limited.

Perhaps such an injury might have deterred a less determined person. But Lloyd worked all the harder.

"The accident accomplished two purposes," he says. "It speeded up a more realistic interpretation of my character. I discarded the flowing tie and any type of costume which differentiated me from the average man of the street.

"The accident also gave me plenty of time to think. And when I found that I had emerged practically unscathed except for my hand injury, I resolved never to forget my good fortune. I don't believe I ever have."

Surgeons are now of the opinion that the screen career of Harold Lloyd, comedian, is not ruined as it was feared would be the case as the result of his recent injuries. Lloyd is in the Methodist Hospital here, suffering from the effects of a bomb explosion of peculiar nature. It occurred in a local photographic studio where Lloyd was posing for lobby display pictures. In his hand he held what was supposed to be a make-believe bomb. The fuse lighted for the exposure and a moment later the actor was on the floor and the windows and roof of the studio were in a thousand pieces.

Lloyd suffered a partly shattered right hand, an injured eye and lacerations of the body. It now is believed, however, he will not be so disfigured that he cannot resume work as a star. The bomb was taken from the comedian's studio "prop" room, and no one can account for its charge of explosives.

SEP 3 1919

Harold Lloyd in typical scene
with Snub Pollard. Hal Roach
is directing. The leading lady
is Bebe Daniels.

Harold Lloyd and Mildred Davis in *Grandma's Boy.*

CHAPTER FIVE

Typical American - Almost . . .

With characteristic energy, Harold Lloyd set out to pick up where he had left off. His Glass Character was becoming more and more a favorite American institution.

"Unlike most comedians, I played a variety of roles—a doctor, a farm boy, a millionaire. It wasn't how I looked, but how I reacted that made me funny," he commented. The fact is that Harold Lloyd was a movie hero who wasn't very much different from most ordinary men. But that small difference was awfully important. If Chaplin was the average man as nonconformist, Lloyd was the average man as conformist.

He did things ordinary men would like to do. He was a typical American man—almost.

He was always on the move. What he lacked in muscle, he

97

inevitably made up in desperation, as his publicity men put it.

There was never a pause in his moving picture career to lament a loss or bewail a frustration, because the next hour, the next minute, there was either a solution or other losses and other frustrations, one coming on top of another in a breathless fashion.

As far back as 1919, a writer interviewing him reported in *The New York Times* that "he seemed like such an erratic person, always jumping up and down on camels or vaulting over something or running away with somebody's wife, but he doesn't do that in real life at all."

It was Harold's aim to develop a character the public could believe in. His antics and adventures were stretched, but never beyond the point of possibility. And there was always that struggle against the bigger man, against the bigger odds, against the impossible. An extrovert to the core, Harold was the young man who would not take no for an answer. Evidently nobody ever told him that anything was impossible. Therefore, he proceeded to do what could not be done.

The American public welcomed Harold's hectic satire on America's young go-getter.

It is improbable, at the time, that Lloyd realized he was satirizing a character who had become "the great all-American youth." He was no more conscious of this than was Mack Sennett of creating a new art form in the world of comedy.

According to Lloyd, "my purpose was to obtain laughs. Whatever else came from my comedies was an extra dividend." The Harold Lloyd brand of humor was closer to Burchard, Nebraska, than to Broadway or Hollywood.

As early as spring of 1920, the newspapers were referring to Harold Lloyd as the nation's "favorite comedian." The Toledo *Blade* reported to its readers that Harold Lloyd "is fast becoming one of the most popular screen comedians. His type of comedy is clean, novel, and funny."

A month later, *The New York Times* reported that "Harold Lloyd, the screen comedian, has become a star of the Associated Exhibitors, Inc. by an arrangement 'involving more than $15,000,000' during the first year of its existence."

98

Back in 1918, on one of Harold Lloyd's rare visits to New York, he discovered his picture *Bumping Into Broadway* playing in a leading theater and his name in lights. The film was retained for three straight weeks.

In the years ahead, Lloyd was to challenge even the box office accomplishments of the great Chaplin and, in certain peak years, even surpass them.

"I was glad to find a character that I could say was truly my own, that was different from all the other comic characters on the stage and screen," says Lloyd. "My character had an individuality. The glasses made him look very studious, but he belied that appearance in the things he did. There would be times when butter wouldn't melt in his mouth.

"I had a comic idea built behind my character. Foremost, he was a human being. He became someone that people would recognize. Everything about him was normal—his shoes, his clothes, the way he walked and talked. He could be the young man living next door. He was like anyone you passed on the street. Millions of people wore glasses and a straw hat. And he wore glasses and a straw hat.

Harold Lloyd---the Happy Comedian

Motion Picture Classic Oct 1919.

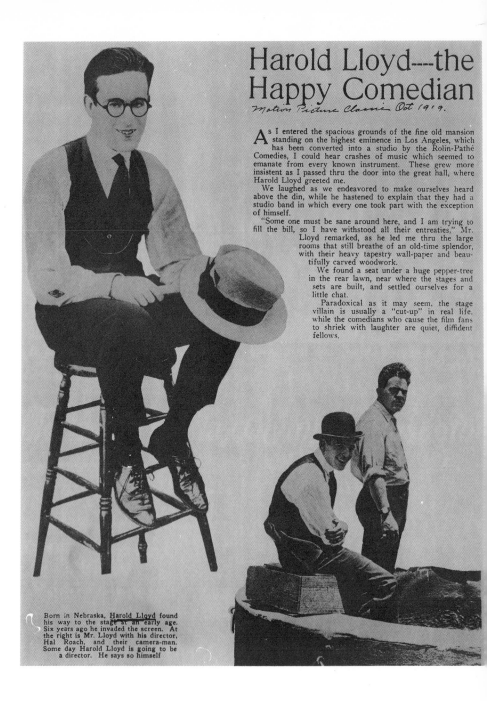

A s I entered the spacious grounds of the fine old mansion standing on the highest eminence in Los Angeles, which has been converted into a studio by the Rolin-Pathé Comedies, I could hear crashes of music which seemed to emanate from every known instrument. These grew more insistent as I passed thru the door into the great hall, where Harold Lloyd greeted me.

We laughed as we endeavored to make ourselves heard above the din, while he hastened to explain that they had a studio band in which every one took part with the exception of himself.

"Some one must be sane around here, and I am trying to fill the bill, so I have withstood all their entreaties," Mr. Lloyd remarked, as he led me thru the large rooms that still breathe of an old-time splendor, with their heavy tapestry wall-paper and beautifully carved woodwork.

We found a seat under a huge pepper-tree in the rear lawn, near where the stages and sets are built, and settled ourselves for a little chat.

Paradoxical as it may seem, the stage villain is usually a "cut-up" in real life, while the comedians who cause the film fans to shriek with laughter are quiet, diffident fellows.

Born in Nebraska, Harold Lloyd found his way to the stage at an early age. Six years ago he invaded the screen. At the right is Mr. Lloyd with his director, Hal Roach, and their camera-man. Some day Harold Lloyd is going to be a director. He says so himself

"Every comedian needed a trademark in those days. A big mustache or a chin piece was necessary. Or he had to be sad or cross-eyed or short or slim or tall. He had to have a characteristic that the public would identify with him. I was, therefore, referred to as the man with the glasses.

"Many comedians looked grotesque. My character didn't look unusual as a rule unless a particular part called for certain funny clothes or a funny hat or something special. As a whole, my character's appearance was almost what we call 'straight.' But while I looked thoroughly normal, suddenly it was revealed that I had a sort of screwy mind. In an unusual situation, I didn't act normally as other young men might. My entire thinking was off on a different tangent.

"For example, if I fought somebody, I didn't fight him as George or John or Bill would do. I fought him in an entirely different manner. It was a manner that many people might have dreamed of using, but wouldn't have dared. And the audience was usually waiting to see what in the world would happen as a result.

"That was the reason why I insisted at the introduction of my character that I put out a one reel picture each week. I wanted the public to become acquainted with my new character. It was only the eccentricities that lay behind the normal appearance of the young man that would win me supporters.

"There was a time when some people began to say, 'Lloyd is only a comedian because of the material he has or the situation comedy he develops.'

"Well, that's not true. If true at all, it's true of all comedians. Every comedian must have material. And he must create situations and conditions. But the character has got to be an innately funny one, yet not necessarily because of his clothes or his face, or the way his hair sticks up, or his short arms or short legs. Sure, they're helpful; but they confine the actor to a certain extent unless he can rise out of it as most of our top comics do.

"My character symbolized something important. I symbolized the little, struggling man, working at menial types of jobs. He might be a soda jerk, a ribbon salesman, or somebody who

101

is trying to get a job. In any event, he was always struggling against the bigger man or the difficult situation. People recognized in this character the things that they wanted and had wanted. He was really no different from anybody else. But he did things that other people would like to have done."

One of the reasons why Harold Lloyd sought a screen personality of the type he was to develop in his Glass Character was that he wanted a believable young man who would not have to stick to slapstick comedy. He wanted a character that could engage in romance on occasion.

"I wanted a character whose romance with girls was believable to the audience. Now when I was Lonesome Luke or one of those other comic characters, love affairs were not real. They were travesties on the real thing. The heroine had to be just as screwy as the hero.

"My new character, however, could participate in little scenes of romance that were entirely devoid of comedy theme. They represented a change of pace. And I had learned from my early theatrical days how important pacing was in establishing real comic moods or receptivity for comedy when it came.

"An example of this was a lovely little scene in one of my pictures where I say good-bye to a girl friend. As she walks away, I climb into the first bough of a nearby tree and wave good-bye to her. She then goes over a hill in the distance, and I climb further into the tree in order to see her and again call out and wave good-bye—this time asking her name. As she goes on further, I climb the tree higher and call to her, 'Where do you live?' She answers and continues on her way, and I climb still higher. At last I reach the very top of the tree in order to wave and call good-bye to her. She waves back and disappears in the distance.

"Well, it is a delightful little love scene. I couldn't have done that and made it believable in a Lonesome Luke comedy. My Glass Character was convincing enough to engage in romance and evoke honest emotions from the audience. That was what I wanted. The majority of comic characters couldn't do that."

102

He was despondent, but only
temporarily.

His determination overcame
all obstacles.

Nothing seemed to faze him.

He did what we all would
like to do.

Women loved him.

And he loved the women.

While he had his
daydreams . . .

He was usually too shy to do
anything about them.

He took life easy . . .

but made heroism seem easy.

He finally got his girl — but sometimes didn't know what to do with her.

Harold Lloyd achieved a blend of slapstick and situation comedy which helped create a new pictorial comedy form for the American film world. Other major comedians such as Harry Langdon, Buster Keaton, and Charlie Chaplin were also following this new trend towards feature films which went beyond the more elemental slapstick techniques of the Mack Sennett period.

Whether it was Harold Lloyd's early training in the shadow of McGuffey teachings, or the rebellion of motion picture audiences against much publicized Hollywood excesses, is difficult to say. But the Lloyd pictures became known as clean pictures which the entire family could see and enjoy. "If there was one thing I was proud of, it was that exhibitors were willing to book my pictures without actually seeing them," says Lloyd.

"There was another thing typical of my comedies. For parties of children or even for a girls' school, *Grandma's Boy*, *Girl Shy*, or any of my pictures were in perfect taste. A great deal of comedy can be obtained from off-color scenes, incidents or gags, and it is giving up something from the producers' point of view to avoid such things. Sometimes easy laughs lay within this area. But we always felt in those days that this was not our approach. There is plenty of comedy around without going in this direction."

"Different as he is," wrote a Hollywood columnist, "he's the strangest, most modest, genuinely liked man in Hollywood." When confronted with the accusation of undue modesty, however, Harold Lloyd once answered a reporter in a newspaper interview, "Don't credit me with modesty. The fact is that I have worked too hard on my own comedies to regard them as laughing matters."

106

Bebe Daniels

Jobyna Ralston

In 1919, Harold Lloyd's leading lady, Bebe Daniels, who had played in 172 Lloyd comedies in four years, received an offer from Cecil B. De Mille. She decided to leave the Harold Lloyd organization. Harold and Roach went in search of a new leading lady.

One night, they happened to see a motion picture called *Weaver of Dreams*. The leading lady in the movie, petite and blonde, seemed to be just the type they were looking for. Her name was Mildred Davis. But she couldn't seem to be located.

Mildred Davis

Above is the first published glimpse o
Mr. Lloyd's new leading woman, Mildre
Davis, who succeeds Bebe Daniels, now
dedicated to the drama. Will Mildre
be another Bebe? We shall see—w
shall see!

After a little detective work, Roach discovered that she had returned to school in Tacoma, Washington. He wired her asking that she report for a screen test. She did, and soon she was acting small parts with Lloyd. After a time, she became his leading lady in such movies as *Safety Last* and *Grandma's Boy*.

One Saturday afternoon in February, 1923, just after *Safety Last* was completed, Harold and his leading lady sneaked off to a small church in Hollywood and were married without benefit of much publicity.

"I married Mid," Lloyd likes to say, "because I found out she was about to leave me to do pictures for somebody else, and I figured that was the only way to keep her around." He has been married to the same girl ever since.

"I've had to think of a lot of ideas in my life," says Harold. "But marrying Mid was one of the best I ever had."

The Glass Character Lloyd created was a typical American young man. But Harold Lloyd, by a peculiar combination of opposites, was also to create one of the most physically daring characters in the history of motion pictures.

The first published glimpse of Harold's new leading lady — Mildred Davis — appeared in a magazine of the day. *Right,* Harold relaxing at his home.

The popularity of Harold Lloyd spread to other countries.

Such was Harold Lloyd's growing popularity that an envelope merely had to have his picture on it to be delivered.

CHAPTER SIX

Daredevil

"I was always amazed at the reactions of my own children when they saw my films," Harold Lloyd recalls. "In almost every picture I made I was always the underdog. I took an awful kicking around, and everybody picked on me. My two girls used to weep and wail, but with the boy it was different. He wanted to battle. He sometimes sat tense with his teeth clenched."

There were good reasons. Few performers have taken such a beating and as many risks as did Lloyd. While elementary safety precautions were always followed, Lloyd usually did not use a double even for performing his most difficult stunts.

"It was not," says Harold, "that I preferred to risk my neck. Or that I was against using a double. It was simply the fact that a double's action did not look like mine or give off the same comic feeling.

"A comedian's art is not just gags and jokes. Every motion, no matter how small, is part of the act. Even the back of the body is expressive. And when a professional double is used, he does not pretend to be either an actor or a comedian, and it often shows. He photographs flat.

"Of course, I used a double for stunts that I obviously couldn't do. Or at least I used a double to do the stunt first; and then I would do it, after studying carefully the way he did it."

Harold was athletically inclined from his early days when he wanted to become a professional boxer. His early film experiences developed his acrobatic abilities so that, as Lonesome Luke, he was often billed as "The Human Rubber Ball." A trade newspaper reviewer, writing about a Lloyd one-reeler, stated: "Harold Lloyd must be made of Indian rubber. The way he suffers himself to be kicked all over the map, hit on the head with a mallet, to fall down a dizzy flight of stairs, is marvelous."

Lloyd became one of the pioneers of "thrill comedy," the kind *Liberty* magazine referred to as "comedies of terror." It was, however, as a "human spider," a human being that climbs the surface of tall buildings, that Harold Lloyd made his chief claim to fame as a thrill comedian. This was so despite the fact that he had climbing sequences in only five out of some three hundred films.

Lloyd's pictures which involved an apparent climb to dizzy heights showed him clawing his way by finger and toe, to spots precarious even for a pigeon. Always there were little ants of people far down below. There were, too, frantic efforts to maintain balance where a slip would plunge our hero to his complete destruction in the abyss below. Expert at building gag upon gag, Lloyd placed one death-defying antic upon another, like so many building blocks, until the audience left the theater, reduced by screams and laughter to one great mass of perspiring, nervous exhaustion.

The first in the series of "human spider" thrillers was *High and Dizzy*, a two-reeler. *Look Out Below*, a two-reeler made in 1920, followed and *Never Weaken*, a three-reeler, was made the year following. His greatest thrill picture, and perhaps his greatest all-around movie, was *Safety Last*, a feature film made in 1923. It was the story of a country boy who comes to the big city and agrees to replace a professional "human fly" in climbing the exterior of a skyscraper.

The naive clerk gets himself into trouble by agreeing to take the place of a "human fly." Crowds of people wish him luck. *Safety Last*, made in 1923, is considered one of Harold Lloyd's best.

During the first few days of filming *Safety Last*, Lloyd says, he was always scared. "I'd have to adjust. After working a few weeks, I would be thoroughly at home at the edge of any roof." Nearly a quarter of the running time of *Safety Last* has to do with Harold's climb. Those were the days before the trick photography and process film development. The illusion lay in the deceptive camera angles of drop in height.

How were the stunts actually accomplished? "In the first place," says Lloyd, "we used four buildings. We picked out a structure we wanted for the actual building. Then we chose a two story, four story, or whatever height building we needed. Then we built our own sets on top of them.

"We started the film with a one-story building and built our set right on the edge of the real building's roof. We built it so that we could put platforms out and constructed the scaffolding on the side so that the camera man could be up there and shoot down. I remember how we had to put the platform low enough and narrow enough so that the camera man could miss it when he was shooting down at an angle.

"The platform would be fourteen feet or so below us. From above it looked no bigger than a postage stamp! It was loaded with mattresses in order to break our fall if we did slip as we went through our antics. We didn't want to commit suicide just to make somebody laugh. But we were always in danger despite this precaution. Falling even a short distance was no small matter. Besides, we could easily roll off the platform because it didn't have any railings around it.

"In those days, we didn't want to divulge how we performed our stunts. We didn't want to give away any of our techniques for fear of making the public disillusioned with the thrill of it all. Looking back, it seems strange that we would have this worry, for the thrills were far from artificial. The danger, while not as great as it might appear to the public, was nevertheless still very real."

Climbing buildings was not the only stunt that made Harold Lloyd one of the most daring comedians of all. His chases were episodes where anything might happen. They were not mere slapstick but had motivation and plot.

Small wonder Lloyd had to train like an athlete for his films.

"All kinds of hazardous incidents would develop as the result of the type of thrill picture we made. For instance, a bus would come between two streetcars just before they crashed together. We couldn't crank our cameras slow enough to speed up the action artificially for fear that the film might appear too jerky. There had to be some amount of actual collision involved in such scenes. And since I usually participated as the hero without a double, there were often instances when I escaped injury only by the closest possible margin.

"In one episode, I was on the rear end of a fire engine as it raced down the street. According to our gag, the hose I was holding was to unwind as I held it, hand over hand. As the hose ran out, it was supposed to be connected at the base. That was to save me from falling off the racing fire truck onto my back. Unfortunately, the hose was not connected. I fell to the street and ended up in the hospital. 'Did it hurt you?' I was asked when I regained consciousness.

" 'It didn't do me any good,' I replied.

"Occasionally, people felt that a double should be used for me in doing some of the more hazardous scenes, particularly those which involved climbing. I was not adverse to this; however, the director would always say, after a double had taken part, that the scene didn't really turn out properly, and the double didn't seem really to look like me. Then the scene would be shot over again, and I would be participating without benefit of assistance! Of course, having the double do the job ahead of time was helpful because I would see how an expert would do it. And this would insure a greater degree of safety than if I were pioneering myself.

"I found it was necessary to keep in top physical condition throughout my motion picture career. I would train for my pictures as a boxer would train for a championship match. During the production of one of my pictures, *The Milky Way*, I lost fifteen pounds.

No matter where he may be, Lloyd wears his inevitable glasses.

Giants, gunmen — they were all part of Harold Lloyd's world of adventure.

"In our street scenes, we learned that we had to have our own automobiles, our own buses, our own streetcars, and all of our own traffic. We had our own pedestrians, too."

No time or money was spared in constructing the basic materials for one of Harold Lloyd's thrill pictures. In his *Professor Beware*, Harold Lloyd played an archaeologist en route to New York, riding atop a freight train, very comfortable and safe. However, as the train approached a tunnel which was full of gas, the hero saw that he must save himself by somehow getting off the moving train. The solution was to run along the top of the moving cars, making huge jumps from one to the next, until he was able to grab hold of an overhanging beam and thus save himself from entering the tunnel.

Even carrying a suitcase, Lloyd could run like a trained sprinter. In order to get the effect of running on the train, he decided to attempt three different methods of photography. One involved using a real train and tunnel, another called for the use of a miniature train and treadmill with moving scenery,

125

and the last involved building a treadmill at eye level with the moving train so that the spectator could not see it located on the other side on a slightly raised hill.

When Harold seemed to be running madly on top of the moving train, he was actually running on the treadmill, parallel with the train. When one car ended and another began, Harold Lloyd would make a long leap on the treadmill. From the point of view of the spectators, it looked as though he were leaping from one car to another.

"It really was very difficult, almost harder than running on the real train, to run on this treadmill," says Lloyd. "We had lines marked on it because I had to jump on the treadmill practically full speed. And, if I fell, there was a risk of serious injury, because the treadmill was going very fast.

"On another occasion, shortly after we had made *Safety Last,* we faced difficulty in having the picture shown in Chicago. At that time, Chicago was tied up with three distributing organizations which had control. They wanted to give us what we thought was an inadequate sum for *Safety Last,* so we decided to try to sponsor the picture in Chicago ourselves. We hired a theater, and I came to Chicago to assist in the promotion.

"When I arrived, I found that they were planning to give me the key to the city. Along with varied ceremonies and nice words, they also had planned to make special use of my so-called building-climbing ability—or at least what they thought was my building-climbing ability. They had arranged for me to christen a clock on the Wrigley Building, which was about fifteen stories high in the air!

"I was told that no one had ever christened the clock before and that this was a wonderful opportunity to promote the picture which showed me to be such a talented human fly. 'If you expect me to do this stunt,' I gasped, 'you'll just have to forget about the whole idea.'

" 'We can't,' I was told. 'Because right now there is a huge crowd of ten thousand people waiting outside the building to see you in action.'

"I went down there, and, sure enough, there was the crowd,

In the film *Professor Beware*, Harold Lloyd appears to run desperately, suitcase in hand, from one speeding express freight car to another, in order to avoid entering a tunnel where poisonous gas threatens. Actually, Lloyd is not running on the freight trains at all but on a treadmill parallel to it. He also did the same scene running on top of a real moving train.

and there was the building. And everyone was awaiting my arrival. I thought, 'My God, is everybody in Chicago here?'

"I finally found that they were not sure that I would do the stunt after all. What they expected me to do was to walk into the building. Inside, they had a professional human fly dressed in my type of clothes with a pair of glasses on, whom they expected to lower in one of those boatswain seats, with a rope over the edge of the building. Then he would make a daring attempt to christen the clock by breaking a bottle of champagne over it.

"However, when the professional human fly saw the force of the gusts that were blowing around the building and the immense dangers involved in the stunt, he simply walked out.

"'What are we going to do now, Harold?' I was asked. 'Would it be possible for you to substitute for the human spider like you do in your movies?'

"At that moment, my secretary stepped up and stated, 'Well, gentlemen, if Lloyd does this, he is going to have all of his insurance canceled on the instant.'

"They turned to me questioningly. There was no doubt in my mind. I was not going to participate in any human fly activities on the Chicago building.

"Instead, I asked for a megaphone and permission to speak to the crowd from the top of an automobile. I told the crowd exactly what had happened, play by play. The story was so funny that the audience roared and took it as a substitute for the deed."

There were other occasions when Harold Lloyd was faced with serious physical problems in his pictures. For example, in *The Freshman*, he played in a football game with professional football players. One of the scenes was a practice session in which the coach used Harold as a tackling dummy. The real dummy was broken and "the freshman" seemed a good substitute.

Being strangled was part of the day's work for Harold Lloyd. Harold Lloyd and William Frawley wrestle in *Professor Beware*.

Dozens of players lined up to tackle Harold. Some of them were professional players and others merely motion picture extras. "When the professional football players tackled me," says Harold, "I didn't feel it because they seemed to know how to tackle without hurting a person. However, when the amateurs hit me, it was really painful. After that scene, I felt sore for a week."

While Harold Lloyd became known as the comedian who climbed buildings and hung from flagpoles, this was only part of his arsenal of humor. He would be dragged, pulled, torn, thrown, hit, and bounced in almost all of his movies. But despite the roughness with which he was treated and the scrapes he got into, he bounced back with amazing agility. This seemingly superhuman ability to triumph over odds delighted the audiences.

It was no accident that Lloyd's Glass Character became one of the most effective laugh-makers in the history of American entertainment. Harold Lloyd worked at it. He had to know what the public would laugh at and what it would not. His success was the result of painstaking effort to build one gag upon the other with proper spacing and timing, all integrated into the comic character which he had created with so much effort.

How this was done is an important part of America's comic tradition.

CHAPTER SEVEN

The Art of Being Funny

Harold Lloyd attributes his success to an unusually large comedy vocabulary.

"Vocabulary is not the right word. But I do not know a better. By it I mean the tools of my trade: the store of knowledge of comedy effects—what they are and how to obtain them —accumulated by long experience and observation and sharpened by a natural instinct for what is funny."

The comedy of Lloyd lies, as he puts it, "in the humor of events, not in any conscious effort of mine to be cute.

"The theater caught me young, and no experience in it— cellar stage, amateur, stock company, stage hand, picture extra, or one-reel slapstick—was wasted. Specialization, plus aptitude, plus work, seemed to be the formula for my advancement in the films.

"I realize this is not exactly new. But these are the ingredients, as I study the situation, that have been most helpful to me."

"Funny *material and knowing* what is funny are just a part of the making of a top-flight comic. Looking funny can get you off to a good start. But it does not sustain. A top comic must have a knowledge of pantomine and how to present his comic ideas in an individual way.

"In other words, it seems to me that the comedian must have within him a natural bent and feeling for humor. He must have this as well as knowledge of what is funny.

"It's difficult to put all this into words. But a comedian must have that certain capacity within himself for funny ideas which may come to him at any time, even while in the middle of a scene. Thus he can add to what he is doing, build on it, and render even funny lines and situations funnier."

Years ago, *The New Yorker* pointed out that Lloyd "has something that . . . others lack—and that is a shrewd, selective intelligence, which enables him to distinguish between the funny and the unfunny. He also possesses an uncanny mastery of pace; whatever else his comedies are or are not, they are always fast on their feet. They start moving toward a definite objective and they gather momentum as they progress."

Few comedians have greater knowledge of the techniques of

132

comedy. The Lloyd formula in the silent days was to think up a good gag or comedy sequence and start filming. There usually was not too much concern about the story.

"The earliest method of comedy construction," says Lloyd, "was to begin with a policeman or policemen to chase your comedian. The rest of the cast was optional, except that there must be a girl.

"We would sometimes get a general idea, a cast to fit it, and a good location, and then we'd start shooting. We often started in mid-picture. We couldn't afford gag men, so Roach and I would usually think up our own ideas.

"We never hesitated to stop the progress of the story or to forget about the story completely in order to shoot a reel of gag sequences. In the early days it was the gag that came first. We would work for as long as we thought necessary and then we would quit for a few days until someone got a new idea.

"Of course, as feature films developed we went far beyond these early techniques and began utilizing more subtle plots and characterizations."

Lloyd has ofen been asked just how he set about making one of his picture successes.

"How do I make a picture?" he once answered, "I don't. It grows like Topsy."

But there was more to it than that. In preparing any of his famous silent feature films, Lloyd had not only youthful enthusiasm, he was also painstaking in every detail. He pored over every aspect of his comedies long before they went into production. No aspect escaped study. "Together with Roach and his gag men, we would construct a picture until he considered it just about as perfect as it could be."

The matter of a title was of special importance. His feature film *Speedy*, for example, featured Lloyd as a dreamer who spent all his time day-dreaming about baseball. The title of the picture came from a nickname given Harold by his father when he was a boy. When an uncle of Harold's insisted on calling him by his proper name, Harold would say, "Don't call me Harold, call me Speedy."

133

"Dad pinned the name on me," Lloyd recalls, "and we became Speedy and Foxy, which was a nickname my father had earned in his youth. When the character of the picture *Speedy* began to take shape, it was seen that the name fitted. Moreover, *Speedy* was brief and suggestive, therefore an intrinsically good title."

While Lloyd's popularity grew, important changes were taking place in the motion picture industry—the baby was growing up. Old-fashioned slapstick one- and two-reelers were giving way to longer feature films.

"What happened to the old comedies?" asked Adolph Zukor,

Camera men filming Harold Lloyd pictures had to take chances too.

the pioneer producer. "I must plead guilty to having been partly responsible for their demise, though inadvertently. The development of the feature picture was the handwriting on the wall. Sennett had started in the day of short films, and his momentum kept him going as the features gradually took over the field. It was not that theater bills lacked room for the comedies. The main trouble was that exhibitors refused to pay a high price for what became a side dish of movie fare. Therefore, the comedians were not able to command high salaries, and inevitably the best of the talent, old and new alike, aimed at the longer pictures."

Influenced both by the developing industry of the nineteen twenties and by his own preferences, Lloyd summed up the situation: "We are now making two-reelers instead of one, and these pictures follow a consistent story with plausible action, definite, building-up scenes, holding suspense and hard interest. We hope to work into a blend which would incorporate light, broad, dramatic, and farcical comedy, as well as slap-

Being a stunt man is no easy life. Pictures opposite show Harold Lloyd clutching the top of a cattle car while below are the sharp horns of steers. The second picture: the anguished face of tiring Lloyd. Picture three: a board placed under Lloyd permits him to rest between shots as the camera crew watches.

How to Get a Laugh *By Harold Lloyd*

THIS funny old world is filled **You Have to Dig for It in M----- -** ----- ---- ---
with several hundred millions

May, 1926

The Ladies HOME JOURNAL

The Hardships of Fun Making

By HAROLD LLOYD

stick. Because the public taste for amusement is slowly undergoing a change, and the old tricks and stunts which have been considered essential are giving way to amusing situations."

Despite the changing pattern of film making, lessons learned in the old slapstick school were remembered by Lloyd, Chaplin, and Keaton throughout their careers.

There was, for example, the "law" of comedy that every comedian must have a trademark, usually a comic mustache, a "mo" as the trade name went, and that it must be distinctive.

"Chester Conklin, one of Mack Sennett's old reliables, used a walrus effect; Chaplin a toothbrush mustache. And the field was pretty much pre-empted. We went to a wig maker in search of a new effect for Harry (Snub) Pollard, and after much looking, he accidently reversed a pair of Kaiser Wilhelm mustachios in trying them on. The result was so absurd and original that we looked no further, and they were Pollard's trademark for many years."

But the slapstick "laws" of comedy, the obviousness, the incredibility, and the laugh-making tricks soon passed their peak of popularity. Some of the comedians realized that. "Frankly," recalls Lloyd, "slapstick comedies had created laugh riots for

In the old days, every comedian had his special physical characteristic. Ben Turpin, his crossed eyes. Stan Laurel, his cry. Charlie Chaplin, his mustache, hat, and cane. Jimmy Durante, his nose. Buster Keaton, his stone face. Edgar Kennedy, his "slow burn."

Even though hats might change, glasses were a permanent part of Harold Lloyd's personality.

people all over the world, and, when I began to produce pictures of a different kind, it was foolish for me to feel that slapstick was passé. But pictures with a logical basis, a foundation of solid story material, needed to get away from the hodgepodge of slapstick. The audience could not be led to expect one brand of comedy and then given another.

"I think the best prescription I can give for success in one type of comedy-producing is to change constantly the type of story in which one appears. Introduce new types of characters and surroundings, and keep your material logical, even though it may stretch the imagination a little. There is a certain formula, but it's not so clear as formulas for baking a cake or making a suit of clothes: one cannot follow a recipe or pursue any set course in laugh-making. What is funny in one situation is incongruous and almost idiotic in another.

"There are certain sure-fire situations, but they cannot be used continuously. An idea used in one picture may meet the expected response. But repeated in another, it's bound to be a miserable flop. Public moods are varied and fickle. One time they run to broad slapstick comedy. The next time the more subtle type of fun appeals most. That is one thing that the successful producer has to watch. He must keep the feel of the public's amusement pulse and anticipate the fluctuation of tastes."

Some observers agree with Joe Franklin, who wrote in *Classics of the Silent Screen:* "Lloyd's great talent lay not so much in being a comedy performer as being a comedy creator. Of course, he dreamed up so much of his own material, he was naturally the best practitioner of his own form of humor, which is breezy personality socked over to its best advantage."

Lloyd is not in full agreement with such views. "Nobody can be a successful comedian," he believes, "by just relying on his material, good as it may be." Lloyd feels that a true comedian must also reflect an inner comic spirit in his personality, in his way of acting, and in his every gesture.

Lloyd also believes that pictures cannot be precisely true to life and be funny. "For, though life can be very funny, the comic incidents are separated by long intervals of dull routine, with moments of drama and tragedy interspersed. Nature usually is a poor continuity writer. A good picture should crowd more comedy into five to eight reels than could happen to most of us in a lifetime.

Harold Lloyd's Glass Character had a way of getting into predicaments and getting out of them. *Right,* a famous sequence from *The Freshman,* in which he goes to a dance in a suit which has been loosely basted by his tailor.

140

 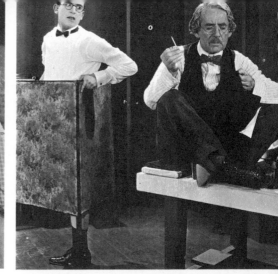

"If it cannot hold a mirror up to life, however, a film comedy can keep within shooting distance of verity. The only test it should pass is: 'Is it plausible while one is looking at it?' It will be so only if the characters themselves are plausible. The actions may be outlandish, but the characters, particularly the central character, must not be. Everyone in the audience should feel that he knows him, has known him, or might easily know him.

"Comedy demands a technique of its own. The big producers have learned that. They once tried to make funny pictures with dramatic directors and failed. Then they called in former comedy directors who had graduated to the larger field. Most dramatic directors cannot time and space comedy, and actors who are accustomed only to dramatic work move too slowly through comedy scenes and fail to underscore their actions properly."

"My comedy was basic," says Lloyd. "There were no language barriers. Take a little boy throwing a snowball at a man and knocking off his top hat—that's basic. Take a fellow slipping on a banana peel—that's basic too."

Among the most famous sequences in all film history is Harold Lloyd's antics with a turkey (from *Hot Water*). *Below*, a sequence, not actually a part of the movie, in which Harold Lloyd is supposed to assassinate a turkey for Thanksgiving; but somehow hasn't the heart to do so.

When one of Harold's first silent moving picture successes, *Bumping Into Broadway*, appeared in New York in 1919, many people thought that he was a brand-new comedian, just arrived in the entertainment world. "They didn't realize the hell I had gone through," says Lloyd. "They didn't realize that I had been on the stage since I was twelve years old; that I had worked in repertory companies and had gone through one-reelers; that I had done Willie Work and Lonesome Luke before I arrived at my Glass Character. They thought I was just a new comedian, born overnight. The hell I was! I had gone through a tremendous schooling and had hard knocks to find out what I should and shouldn't do. Of course, one never exactly learns what he shouldn't do, but it pays to notice the sign posts along the way.

"For example, a comedian is not supposed to let the audience think he believes his comedy is funny. He can't laugh at himself. We occasionally have a great comedian, like Red Skelton, who laughs at his own jokes and gets away with it. But he is the exception.

"Some people used to say that I was funny because I knew how to construct a gag or a situation. But they overlooked the idea that my Glass Character was inherently funny in the way he thought and the way he reacted. If I ran, I ran with a funny, screwball way to make it funny. If I talked, I did it in my own special way. I was an individual with characteristics all my own. And I had to forego the advantage of a lot of gags because I wanted to retain the consistency of the character I had built up.

"It was early in the development of my Glass Character that I realized I must not go into a lot of cartoon-type stuff. In other words, I very seldom did a gag that couldn't be done in real life, at least with a stretch of the imagination."

Similarly, Lloyd never permitted his writers—and he had talented ones, including Sam Taylor and Fred Newmeyer—to engage him in gags about his glasses. He assumed that the glasses were part of his features; he never referred to them or appeared without them. Lloyd comments, "I never used my glasses to draw special attention to them. They were like my nose, my mouth, my eyes. They were something that was part

144

of me. I never took my glasses off. I don't think my audiences ever saw a picture of Harold Lloyd without his glasses. If I was to play a girl, I played a girl with glasses. If I was to play a Civil War soldier, I had my glasses adapted to give the feeling of a century ago." (See frontispiece.)

"So, when I played football, people didn't give a thought to it that I wore my glasses. Even when I went in swimming, I had my glasses on. When I was in bed, I had them on too. People accepted the glasses as part of my screwball type of character.

"There was a scene in one of my pictures where people were stepping on my face, and generally giving me a going over. The audience didn't stop to think, 'Oh, his glasses will be broken!' They just didn't think of my glasses as separate from my own personality."

Without his glasses, Harold was no longer Harold Lloyd, the famous screen personality. "There was more magic in a pair of horn-rimmed glasses than the opticians dreamed of," says Harold. "With them, I was Harold Lloyd. Without them I was a private citizen. I was able to stroll unrecognized down any street in the land at any time without the glasses, a boon granted to few other motion picture actors, and one for which some of them would pay quite well."

"Underneath it all," Lloyd stated in an interview with Professor Arthur B. Friedman, of the University of California, "I do think that to rise above the ordinary strata of comedy you've got to be a student of comedy and know what basic ideas you're trying to project in the comedy line and the humorous end. In other words, you'll find a lot of people, both men and women, who are very funny and very amusing in the ordinary walk of life. People laugh at them and say, 'Oh, you should be on the stage.'

"Well, take that particular person—I don't say there aren't exceptions to the rule—take that particular person and chances are strong that he'll be quite different in front of an audience. The audience just doesn't seem to catch the quality of humor the intimate group has found. On stage, the comic has to have a routine, and, when he must give a whole act, it becomes another thing. Many people tighten up."

145

A film critic of the period once wrote, "It is said in Hollywood that Lloyd's is the most efficient and sensibly constructed production unit in the movies. There is good reason for this. Lloyd is, above all things, humble and lacking in ostentation. He has made friends with the men with whom he has worked, and on whom he has depended; he has never lorded it over them. As a result, they are all dedicated to one single purpose in life: the putting over, with a bang, of Harold Lloyd."

But even this was to prove insufficient to withstand the results of a mightier "bang," about to resound throughout the film industry.

Harold Lloyd's famous "used car" sequence from *Hot Water*.

W. C. Fields and Mae West.

CHAPTER EIGHT

The Sound of Comedy

The coming of talkies in 1928 raised serious questions as to whether laugh-makers—expert in visual gags and pantomime—could adapt their art to the uses of sound.

But there was no dodging the issue. Talking pictures had taken over the movie business throughout the country.

A year later sound films were made almost exclusively. New comic talent was imported from vaudeville, burlesque, and Broadway musical comedy theater. Wherever possible, established film stars were trained in the new medium. However, when voices and temperaments did not lend themselves to the changeover, careers came to a sudden end.

"Some film historians have claimed that sound killed the Golden Age of Comedy," says Harold Lloyd. "That is partly true. But sound didn't actually kill our kind of comedy; sound divorced it.

149

"Sound was an added element that could have enhanced comedy. But technical problems often interfered. Sound equipment was rather crude in those days. Stage techniques were used because performers had to remain close to the microphone. Sound tended to freeze actors and actresses in place. This created special problems for the comedian who depended largely upon physical comedy for his laughs." Years of technological progress had to pass before the sound camera was to be freed from its initial enthrallment.

"Most of the early talkies were made on cumbersome sound stages," says Lloyd, "and very little action was possible. When production went outdoors, there were all kinds of problems, including extraneous noises, such as passing airplanes.

"Comedy became a verbal medium, depending on jokes instead of pantomime, mimic, or sight gags. In those days, producers found it cheaper for comedians just to tell jokes, rather than to go out with sound equipment and try for action.

"Our silent comedies had, of course, been basically *motion* pictures. Action was everything! They couldn't have been done on the stage or in any other medium. But the new comedies, including many fine ones, could usually have been done in stage production. Up to the coming of talkies, we never used a bona fide script—just notes!

"I doubt that the movies can ever go back to the sight comedy that we did in the old days. You don't have sight gag men. You don't have the schools of vaudeville and burlesque or two-reel comedies in which to train comics."

Symbolically, Mack Sennett retired in 1933. His era was over. The crown of comedy king was to be taken over by Walt Disney, whose productions were to gross more than $8,000,000 by 1953 and $74,000,000 ten years later.

With the inception of the talkies Charlie Chaplin was faced with a dilemma. His character, the little tramp, was essentially a pantomimic character. When his famous picture *Modern Times* was made in 1936, it was silent except for sound effects.

Chaplin realized that the character he had built into a world favorite faced problems in an era of talk. In 1940, Chaplin

150

finally consented to making a sound picture, *The Great Dictator*, which marked the final appearance of the little tramp character, except for isolated instances. A different Chaplin was to emerge.

Stan Laurel and Oliver Hardy were two of the few major comedians to survive—almost intact—the coming of sound. The transition to talkies was least difficult for them. As Professor McCabe points out in his study of Laurel and Hardy, "there was hardly any difference between their last silent two-reels and their early sound two-reelers." Sound was present; but it was an adjunct to basic sight-comedy techniques. Many comedians felt that the arrival of sound presented the need to *tell* jokes rather than act them out. Laurel and Hardy were fortified with the knowledge that in the movies the theater rule is reversed—the visual takes precedence over the audio. They utilized sound; they were not ruled by it.

Harold Lloyd, together with various film dignitaries, breaking ground for a studio to meet the needs of the new talking picture era. To Lloyd's left and right are Hugh and Charles Christie, famous makers of silent comedies. Howard Hughes is on the extreme right.

Buster Keaton survived the coming of sound, too. "The talkies did not wreck my career," he states. *"Free and Easy,* the first talkie I starred in, was among the biggest money-makers of the year."

Other comedians from the silent screen also kept their jobs, but many veteran laughmakers were imported from Broadway. Jimmy Durante, beloved comedian of night clubs and vaudeville, starred in numerous talking motion pictures. So did Will Rogers, the Ziegfield Follies cowboy comedian. Marie Dressler, a star of both the theater and silent motion pictures, made the transition to talkies successfully.

W. C. Fields, world-famous juggler and a Ziegfeld featured entertainer, was an outstanding comedian in the new films. "The talkies brought one great comedian," says James Agee, "the late, majestically lethargic W. C. Fields, who could not possibly have worked as well in silence; he was the toughest and the most warmly human of all screen comedians."

While Fields was a master pantomimist, his special brand of comedy, backed up by a droll, nasal-speaking voice, proved to be especially effective in the talking films. Although his basically physical comedy and use of visual gags did not depend completely on sound, nevertheless he proved to be at home in the new realm of sound. He wrote and starred in many films, including *You Can't Cheat an Honest Man,* which he authored under the name of Charles Bogle; *The Bank Dick,* which he wrote under the name of Mahatma Kane Jeeves; and *Never Give a Sucker an Even Break,* written under the name of Otis Criblecoblis.

The coming of talking motion pictures made it more difficult for Charlie Chaplin *(upper left)* to continue with his "little tramp" character. He is shown with Martha Raye in *Monsieur Verdoux.* Will Rogers and Jimmy Durante were two Broadway comedians who made good in Hollywood.

153

"I'm travelling a little light," says **W. C. Fields**, the transparent fraud. "The country is fraught with marauders. I'll give you my personal I.O.U. A thing I seldom give to strangers."

"Bill Fields was one of the greatest comedians of any era," says Harold Lloyd. "I often played golf with him. When he finished the ninth hole, he had to have his snort. And he wasn't happy to have his snort alone. I drink very little, but he would go into the locker room and say, 'Come on, Harold, take one.'

"Well, I'd take a couple of swigs. And by the time I got out there on the course again, everything was uphill, believe me. But it didn't seem to bother Bill.

"Bill Fields was always funny, both on and off the camera. He played the role of a cantankerous old character. I remembered him first from the Ziegfeld Follies. He was originally a great juggler, but he began to go in more for comedy. He always had that way of talking out of the corner of his mouth. It was the perversity of Fields, I think, that was one of his major comedy attributes.

"There was also a spontaneous feature about Fields. You never were quite sure what he was going to do. His talking and verbal jokes were second to his physical humor. Many of his jokes were throw-aways, scarcely audible. He was always juggling something, and there was a certain fascination in just watching his walk or the way he carried his cane and wore his hat.

"With children, for example, he was always funny. He built a character of disliking children, of being frightened of them. He would treat them nice when the mother was around; butter wouldn't melt in his mouth. But when Mother turned her back, he would, like as not, give the children a kick in the behind. Or he would be about to do so when the mother suddenly would return and catch him in the act.

"Perhaps that illustrates the strange attractiveness of Bill Fields. A lot of people would like to give troublesome children a swift kick. But none of us dares. When a child gets into mischief, who among us wouldn't want to do what Bill Fields did?

"Bill was a foxy old character, too. He was always a little ingenious and clever in the way he got back at the world for making life miserable for him. He was always trying to outwit other people. And he was always getting into difficulty. But he would finally get the best of it. There was more to his character than that, of course, and he had good material."

Another import from Broadway to Hollywood was the Marx Brothers. "The Marx Brothers came to the movies in the talking period," says Lloyd. "They couldn't have come in the silent era. Groucho is the central character of the team, and Groucho's humor is, primarily—I wouldn't say, completely—verbal. Of course, Harpo is just the opposite. They made him into a dummy because they didn't want him to speak; so he worked purely through pantomime. Chico was a kind of a mixture of the two; there was a phlegmatic quality about him. He used to play his Italian character with the little caricature hat and clothes. And he was musical, too, as was Harpo. He played the piano beautifully, as Harpo played the harp. Zeppo, the fourth Marx Brother, was the straight man.

The Marx Brothers represented a combination of visual and verbal comedy at its wildest. Here is Groucho being shot out of a cannon in *At the Circus*.

"Most of the great motion picture comedians developed characters which didn't need straight men. The entire cast became, in a sense, their straight men. But the Marx Brothers had a zany, almost cartoonish type of comedy. They could do practically anything they wanted in a screwball way. One of the Marx Brothers would be doing one thing and another something entirely different. Their characters were completely different and actually unrelated one to the other.

"Much of the humor of the Marx Brothers, of course, was extremely broad. Groucho was often dry and subtle in his remarks. But the sum total of the Marx Brothers humor was wild, zany, and broad in the tradition of that type of laugh-making. And all of the brothers with the exception of Zeppo, the straight man, required some type of 'mo' or get-up or costume which was completely in the tradition of the early type of film comedians. Harpo had his wig, his pantomimic gags, and his horn-blowing. Groucho had his painted-on mustache and strange way of talking.

"As a matter of fact, Groucho is one of the few comedians who capitalized on glasses in his comedy make-up. His use of glasses was different from mine. His eyeglasses tended to be part of a clown's costume, together with his painted eyebrows, mustache, and cigar. My use of glasses was something quite different. I attempted to utilize glasses in the most acceptable, non-comic manner. They became part of my normal appearance."

The book *Life with Groucho*, by Arthur Marx, discusses Groucho's shift to television: "What a racket this straight acting is!" says Groucho. "Anyone can do it. It doesn't take any talent at all. When you come out on the stage in funny clothes and funny make-up, the audience unconsciously sets up a resistance to you. Right away their attitude is, 'So you're a comedian? Well, let's see how funny you can be. Go ahead. Make me laugh. I dare you to.'

"But, when you come out in street clothes and look like a normal human being, they don't expect to be in the aisles at the first word you say. When you do say something funny, they're pleasantly surprised and laugh all the harder."

"This brought out a theory that he had had for a long time," Arthur Marx comments, "that being a slapstick comic was the toughest work of all."

The Marx Brothers' motion pictures reflected a very heavy reliance on spontaneity, and some of their funniest gags emerged in the production rather than the writing. One such was the stateroom scene from *A Night at the Opera*. The famous episode shows some twenty people squeezed into a tiny ocean liner cabin. With all crowded in the one room, Groucho is busy trying to order his dinner from room service, a plumber is repairing a leak in the pipes, and Harpo and Chico are getting a manicure—all at the same time.

Such a scene couldn't possibly be worked out before an audience. "We weren't like other comedians," says Groucho. "We had to try everything out first. Otherwise, we didn't work well together."

Most of the laugh-makers who survived on film managed to carry over the best tradition of the silent motion pictures into the new medium.

Harold Lloyd was one such comedian who made the transition to talking motion pictures with a minimum of difficulty. His voice was pleasant; his ability to adapt himself to verbal as well as silent visual gags was adequate. His popularity did not waver.

Welcome Danger, made in 1929, was his first talkie. "It was shot first as a silent film," says Lloyd, "and almost released. But we decided to do over a large part of it with dialogue. Of course, the new medium helped us tremendously."

After that came such talkies as *Feet First,* which reminded audiences of the famous silent film *Safety Last;* and *Movie Crazy,* in which Harold, as a shy, movie-struck youngster, falls in love with a moving picture star.

But his early sound films seemed unsatisfactory to Lloyd. They had plenty of hilarious gags, but they were "inadequate for the era of sound motion pictures."

He realized that talking pictures made new demands on the comedian. "You can't keep making pictures following the same formula. You must keep finding new approaches."

Up to that point, Lloyd had built his popularity mostly on his Glass Character and ability to utilize gag situations. The story was secondary to gags and humorous incidents. His popularity had developed from, among other talents, his amazing ability to utilize these gags, building one on top another, with sensitive spacing and timing. The audience was kept laughing almost continuously. He had also created a definite character on the screen with his horn-rimmed glasses and his likable way of going about things. But the sight gag was supreme.

"We had always used some kind of plot in our pictures," Lloyd states. "Some kind of theme was always needed to hang our gags on. But the theme was usually a very thin one. However, in 1934, we decided to make the plot the most important part of our next picture because we took a special fancy to a story by the well-known writer Clarence Budington Kelland."

Harold thought he saw the opportunity for making a movie of Kelland's *The Cat's Paw*. With a few adjustments, the story was thus utilized as the scenario.

The plot had to do with the son of an American missionary in China who returns to his home town and runs for mayor on a so-called reform platform supported by racketeers. Everyone is surprised when the hero actually puts through reforms despite all obstacles.

"In seeking to try something new, we obtained the rights to *The Cat's Paw*, which I had read and admired. I thought it had within it an ideal character for me. Furthermore, I thought that we should try to make this picture in a slightly different way, if we were to retain Kelland's special quality. We weren't sure it would be as popular as the pictures we had been making, but we wanted to keep alert to new ideas and methods.

"Although there were to be plenty of gags and funny situations in *The Cat's Paw*, placing special importance on the story was a little new to Sam Taylor, my director at the time, and all of us."

Not knowing for sure whether this innovation should be undertaken or not, Lloyd decided to let fate decide. He put two pieces of paper in a hat. One was marked "new way" and the other "old way."

"We drew out 'new way,'" recalls Lloyd. "If we had drawn out 'old way,' we would have stuck to our old manner of doing it. And we had worked out in detail how we could handle the story in our traditional manner, if the decision went in that direction."

"*The Cat's Paw* was a success all right," says Lloyd. "But, as I look back, while so many people liked the way the film appeared, I personally think we might have made a better picture if I had drawn out the slip marked 'old way.' So you see how difficult it is to decide such matters."

The picture represented emphasis on plot with gags tailored to fit. Another such film effort was *The Milky Way*. Released in 1936, this film featured a timid milkman who, through a series of confusing incidents, finds himself in line for the middleweight championship of the world. The film was later reproduced as *The Kid From Brooklyn,* featuring the talented comedian Danny Kaye.

When motion picture sound was first introduced, Harold had said, "I can only hope that when the time comes, I shall not try to fool either the public or myself, but will bow my way out as gracefully as I can." With the release of *Professor Beware,* in 1938, Harold realized that his films, though financially successful, no longer satisfied him as they had during the era of silent pictures.

Certain parts of *Professor Beware* pleased him. But the job had been rushed and it showed, to Harold's sensitive eye.

He vowed not to start another picture unless it aroused some of his old-time enthusiasm. From time to time, ideas and stories were examined, but the enthusiasm was not there. Meantime, other interests were receiving Lloyd's attention, many others. So many, in fact, that, without plan or design, the famed name of Harold Lloyd began to become only a happy memory to motion picture viewers around the world.

The appearance of Harold Lloyd in *The Cat's Paw* represented a change in his approach to moving pictures. This film placed major importance on the story rather than the gags.

Harold Lloyd and family. *Left
to right,* Harold, Peggy, Harold
Lloyd, Jr., Mildred, and Gloria.
This picture was taken in the
early 1940's.

CHAPTER NINE

Farewell to Films

Harold Lloyd had been more fortunate than many other stars of the silent screen. When talking pictures took over, he was able to make the transition. The pictures he made, starting with *Welcome Danger*, were as popular and laugh-provoking as his silent films.

But in 1938, when Lloyd finished *Professor Beware*, he felt that somehow the fun had gone out of picture-making. He wanted to find better stories than films such as *Professor Beware*. "I wanted ideas that had the qualities of *Safety Last, Grandma's Boy, The Freshman*, or *The Kid Brother*. I was looking for such ideas. And somehow I just didn't find them. That was the main reason why I find myself turning to things other than making films."

There were, of course, other reasons. The early silent films had, as Paul Rotha states in his book on the films, "a roughness about them, an intensity of feeling, and an air of honesty that have long since vanished in the up-to-date slickness of the Hollywood movie." Or perhaps it was merely that Harold Lloyd had grown older.

Lloyd's training, his greatest ability, and his most spectacular success dated back to silent films. He had made good in talkies; but his heart probably lay in a past era. In his case, there were no compelling financial reasons why he must continue.

Among Harold's homespun American virtues had always been a native shrewdness in matters pertaining to money. He had started out in films with Roach as a wage earner. As he progressed as a comedian he received one-fourth interest in

164

the company, which was subsequently raised one-half. With Harold Lloyd's sudden boom in popularity, Roach had indicated that he didn't think he deserved more than a quarter interest. In 1923, Roach and Lloyd parted amicably.

"Some of the fondest memories in my entire career," says Lloyd, "date back to my association with Roach. There was a close bond between us. I doubt that any two people could understand each other better. As time passes my feeling of indebtedness to Hal Roach grows."

The first picture of the Harold Lloyd Corporation in 1924 was the successful *Girl Shy*. From that time on there was one money-maker after the other. And the money made was largely invested conservatively and without income tax problems.

Starting back in 1916, Harold Lloyd had made, as mentioned before, some three hundred silent and talking pictures. He owned the rights to all but a few. It was estimated that Lloyd films had produced a total gross of some $30 million. In 1927, *Variety* called him one of the "twenty wealthiest showmen of the country."

His earnings were estimated to have exceeded those of Mary Pickford, Douglas Fairbanks, Charlie Chaplin, Gloria Swanson, or any other single motion picture performer in the Golden Age of the Screen.

Symbolic of Lloyd's affluence is the thirty-two-room, Italian Renaissance home, which he built on twenty acres in Beverly Hills. Known as Green Acres, it was equipped with golf course, swimming pools, handball and tennis courts, adjoining buildings, forests, and fountains—about five city blocks in all. Small wonder it became one of the show places of Southern California.

When the Lloyds entered their home for the first time, according to Harold, they "looked at each other and said, 'What are we—damn fools? What did we do? This place is overpowering.'

"But you know," says Harold, "within a week the place began to shrink and to become familiar. We have lived in it ever since and loved it. There are even places where you know the dogs have been."

Part of Lloyd's twenty-acre estate. *Left,* a vase valued at four thousand dollars which graces the rear entrance of the Lloyd mansion. Imported from Italy, the Capo di Monte is considered one of the finest of its type in the world.

Originally, the property was purchased by Harold from a man by the name of Benedict. According to Lloyd, this canyon was named for him. "Joe Schenck and Mary Pickford both wanted the site, but he didn't want to sell. Finally he changed his mind, and my realtors asked me if I wanted to build on it. My first reaction was no. But then we began to fall in love with the place."

Despite accumulated wealth beyond his boyhood dreams, Harold somehow remained relatively unspoiled. When a reporter from the *New York World-Telegram* returned from a visit to the Lloyd home, he wrote, "Harold Lloyd lives more like a king than anyone in Hollywood—yet he does less to emulate that royal person than anyone you know of. All his enviable possessions have done nothing to change those interests and feelings he had as a boy. . . . He is . . . an excellent sportsman, but he will not, just as he wouldn't as a kid, fish or hunt, because he will not kill anything that lives. He won't even have a deer's head in his library."

One magazine said, "It would take more than a vast wealth and boundless fame to effect any serious alterations in the pleasant personality of Harold Lloyd."

For Harold, the world of sports was a constant solace for his pent-up energies. In earlier days, when he was active in films, he would go on a strict routine, running five or six miles each day, playing squash, handball, tennis, and golf as rigorously as a college athlete. When he stopped making movies, even though forty-six years old, he continued his athletic interests.

None but a professional athlete, while a guest at the twenty-acre showplace estate, has been able to follow him around the nine-hole golf course, with its nineteen water hazards, through a few furious games of handball, into the pool for a brisk swim, and then out for some snappy sets of tennis. Afternoons, while guests are recuperating from this sort of routine, Lloyd usually excuses himself and goes bowling. Sometimes he bowls all afternoon and most of the night.

Harold Lloyd's zest for hobbies made retirement easier. A subject would absorb him, and he would apply himself wholeheartedly to it. Invariably, he would become expert. There were mind reading, magic, art, bacteriology, photography, bowling, handball, microscopy, golf, color research, the raising of great Danes, stereophotography, and many others. Lloyd did not dabble. He poured himself into his hobbies as he had his work in films.

One of his favorite pastimes was painting. Rooms of his great house were filled with paints and easels with which he worked. For a long time, he wouldn't display his works about the house; they would hang in his own suite of rooms or in his dressing room at the studio. Later he agreed to a one-man show, which attracted considerable interest.

Entranced by bacteriology, Lloyd acquired two of the finest microscopes in the country. He has read countless books published for medical students and put his information to practical use. "The microscopes opened up a new world for me," Harold once stated. "I was only partially aware before that there were so many fascinating things in nature which are not apparent to the naked eye. Most people don't realize it, but an ant, which you might glance at and forget, is enough for countless evenings' study under the lenses."

A.B.C. TOURNAMENT
Los Angeles Calif.

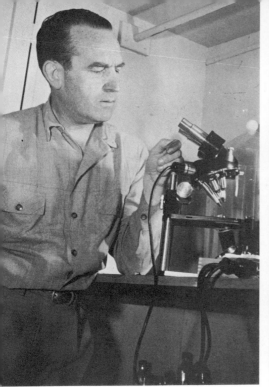

Lloyd approached his hobbies with the same intensity as he did his film-making. He has been a champion bowler, an enthusiastic raiser of dogs, a devotee of microscopy, and a championship handball player. *Right,* Harold and his wife are shown studying color, which has been one of his long-time interests.

Lloyd became such an expert in stereophotography that one of his articles in *Photography* magazine was announced on the cover.

"I'm loaded with hobbies," Lloyd once pointed out. "There definitely is a bit of a scientist in me. I discovered it for sure while making the picture *Professor Beware,* in which I was an archaeologist."

Harold Lloyd refused to accept the word "retirement." "Retirement isn't the word," he said. "I just got to doing other things and stopped making pictures—that was all. My efforts went on in other directions, and I no longer looked for material for films."

When Lloyd found himself with more time on his hands than before, he did not get involved in what might be the usual pursuits of a famous celebrity. He made few speaking appearances at banquets. He appeared in no Broadway shows and seldom on radio. His public appearances were rare, even with the coming of television. And since he owned the rights to practically all of his films, they were not available for public showing except in a few museums.

One special activity claimed a large portion of Lloyd's attention: a Masonic organization, the Shriners. He had joined the Masons with his father back in 1924. From 1949 to 1950, Harold served as Imperial Potentate of the Shriners, the first performer ever to be so honored. He was installed at Soldiers Field Stadium in Chicago before President Harry S. Truman and a crowd of ninety thousand.

During his tenure, he visited Shrine temples in cities throughout the country, participated in parades, and talked to the sick and crippled in all of the seventeen Shrine hospitals.

"And if you think it is easy to travel to more than one hundred communities in a year and to make up to as many as eight speeches a day at these various communities, you're mistaken," says Lloyd. At first it was particularly difficult for Harold, who once had been as ill at ease as his famous screen character when making a public appearance.

"I visited something like 130 cities during the year," says Lloyd. "That doesn't sound like very many, but just get out and try it. Of course, in some places I made several speeches. I spoke in baseball parks and before Congressional bodies, in hospitals, churches, armories—every place."

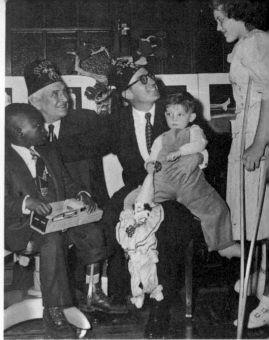

Lloyd was the first entertainer elected Supreme Imperial Potentate of the Shriners, a Masonic order. *Left,* he is shown in 1950 at a huge Shriners' meeting in Soldiers Field, Chicago. *Above,* Harold Lloyd with another famous Shriner, Harry S. Truman; and in one of his frequent visits to hospitals for crippled children when he was an active Shrine leader.

There was something fitting about Harold Lloyd becoming head of such an organization as the Shriners. As *Time* magazine pointed out, "The average Mason comes close to being the average United States male—a hardy fellow with an inner loneliness which he can't quite define. He is anxious to share in good works. United States Masonry supports some 4,500 of its aged brethren and their wives in 30 homes, also supports homes for some 1,400 orphans and needy children." During Harold Lloyd's official service, the Shriners spent some $8,000,000 on hospital operation each year.

Thirteen years later, in 1963, Lloyd was again to be honored by the Shriners when elected president of the Shriners Hospital Corporation and chairman of the board of trustees of the Shriners Hospitals for Crippled Children.

173

Hal Roach, Harold Lloyd, and the late Mack Sennett, many years after they helped make most of the world laugh. Roach is still active today.

On a few occasions, Lloyd has been lured back into motion pictures, once to become a producer for RKO. One of his pictures was *A Girl, a Guy and a Gob,* produced in 1941, and another, *My Favorite Spy,* in 1942.

It was not until 1947, however, that he was actually convinced that he should return to the films as an actor. Howard Hughes, the financier, and the late Preston Sturges, the actor and director, persuaded him to appear in a film called *The Sin of Harold Diddlebock,* released under the title of *Mad Wednesday.*

"The story of *Mad Wednesday,*" says Lloyd, "is that of a young fellow who had become a hero in college. Actually, it opens with the final section of my picture *The Freshman.* Although an important alumnus, the hero is given a job which turns out to be a completely menial bookkeeping task. I stay with this job for twenty years or so, and, after becoming a senior bookkeeper in my declining years, I am fired. I am given a gold watch and some savings. By that time, I have lost all my initiative.

174

"During all these years, the ex-football hero has stopped thinking. He no longer is conscious of the world around him. So when he is fired, he doesn't know what to do. The world startles and frightens him. Then he is talked into taking his first drink. When he does this, things become blotted out, and he gets himself into a lot of trouble. In order to get himself out of this trouble, he has to start thinking again. And when he begins thinking, he returns to his original character.

"Now, that's a lovely story. The theme of the story—the fight against the smugness which comes from security—is a very fine theme. But the way it turned out didn't please me."

The experiment with *Mad Wednesday* was a disappointment to Harold. While he liked the first third of the film, the later two-thirds were made against his better judgment. The humor seemed to him to be exaggerated and in poor taste, the character poorly drawn. Visual gags were second place to spoken dialogue. He wished he had never returned to film-making.

But he was increasingly conscious of the drift of the motion picture industry away from the fun and entertainment of the old days. He wondered how his famous films of a bygone era would be received by today's audiences. He was tempted occasionally to release a film for television use but restrained himself. "The time may come," he said.

In the meantime, he studied the comedians of the present day. And he had decided opinions about them.

An older Harold Lloyd, still resembling the youthful hero, in a scene from *Mad Wednesday*.

Red Skelton.

CHAPTER TEN

Who's Funny Now?

"**M**y feeling is that today we need less 'sick' pictures and more healthy ones," says Harold Lloyd. "I am sometimes astonished at the kind of movies that are being shown.

"Our business in the so-called Golden Age of Comedy was to build for family entertainment. One used to be able to take the whole family to almost any movie. Now it takes good judgment to find even one children should see. It seems to me that we've got to get back to family movies."

Of course, Lloyd's voice is not the only one being raised in criticism of many motion pictures today. John Ford, the film producer, has referred to them as "a market for sex and horror." In the United States, which once rocked the world with laughter, critics point to the lack of comedy films. "Anyone who has watched screen comedy over the past ten or fifteen years," says James Agee, "is bound to realize that it has quietly but steadily deteriorated."

"As far as funny movies are concerned," Abe Burrows, the humorist, once said, "I think that fellows who make the movies now don't risk anything any more. So you've got to make the big picture, and the big picture must be historic, big, serious, romantic. And if it is comic, it is considered light. Where is all the comedy now? You know, it is like saying, 'Where is all the land in New York?' Well, it is under buildings, you know."

Substantiating this claim, Stanley Shapiro, well-known film comedy writer, says that "many producers have built up a resistance to comedy because they are afraid they do not know what is funny, and they do not want to admit it. They seem to think that it might be un-American to admit that they are not experts in comedy."

A. H. Weiler puts it bluntly in *The New York Times*: "The producers have deposited a mere baker's dozen of mirth-provoking movies in local houses during this year of grace (1963), most of them, sadly enough, from abroad. . . . Great comedy, like a fine poem, demands dedication, but its appeal, unlike many serious subjects, is universal and rewarding and often a cheaper proposition for the producer. . . ."

While critical of many of today's films, Harold Lloyd believes that a number of today's comedians are trying to carry on the great tradition of comedy.

"I can think of several great modern women comedians right off the bat," says Lloyd. "Carol Burnett is one. The first time I saw Carol I didn't care for her at all. I thought she was too direct. But I have seen her more often recently, and in my estimation, she has made tremendous strides in knowing where she wants to go 'broad' and where she wants to 'shade' it. Now she has developed a tremendous feeling of finesse. I think she is definitely one of the very top women comedians.

"And then take Judy Holliday. She is splendid! A wonderful comedienne. I think, too, that Shirley McLaine has an excellent feeling for comedy. So has Martha Raye. These are a few who come to mind and fall into the category of great women comedians of my day—such as Marie Dressler and Mabel Normand.

"Now take Lucille Ball. I think she is a great comedienne by any standard and at any time. I don't believe that we have had a comedienne that surpassed her for sheer comic understanding, timing, and ability to handle comic slapstick in the traditional manner. She has a wealth of natural talent."

Lucille Ball is one of the great comediennes of motion pictures and television. A scene from *A Girl, a Guy and a Gob,* the motion picture that Harold Lloyd helped direct in 1941.

Lucille Ball has her own special views about comedy. "Here, at Desilu, we're activating a factory to get as far away from 'sick' comedy and 'sick' comedians as possible. I've never enjoyed this type of comedy—if you call it that—especially when it capitalizes on the afflicted. Our comedy at the studio will continue to be wholesome, i.e., family situations, song and dance, romance, glamour girls, clowns, etc."

Lucille remembers the days when Harold Lloyd was, albeit briefly, a producer. She recalls her experiences with Lloyd: "I admire truly professional people, not only as an observer but as a co-worker. You learn from them. I learned a lot from Harold Lloyd in a motion picture we made called *A Girl, a Guy and a Gob.* Watching him every day on the set was an inspiration. His quiet, reassuring knowledge of his art and how to get the job done was something that stuck with me.

"His authority and understanding, coupled with his great vitality, is what made him one of the greatest comedians of our time. His incomparable timing, his awareness of material, his enchanting quality of being able to develop what I call a 'sense of play,' and his ability to execute them all with a complete credibility, are all the things that made Harold Lloyd a giant among giants."

Carol Burnett.

Another motion picture performer in the comic tradition is Red Skelton. Of him, Buster Keaton remarks: "Red Skelton is a contemporary comedian whose working methods are closest to what ours were in the silent days."

Lloyd agrees. "Red Skelton is one of the great clowns of our time. He not only is able to be supremely funny through his handling of spoken lines and anecdotes, but his physical type of comedy is a throwback to the days of slapstick and Mack Sennett at their best. Red is a physical clown and a great pantomimist. He is able to make people laugh even when he says nothing. His gestures, his facial expressions, his acrobatics, the way he manages to build rapport with his audience even in the difficult medium of television, establish him as one of the great laugh-makers that I know."

"Red Skelton has developed his own style," continues Lloyd. "Skelton could easily have worked in the same period as Chaplin, Keaton, Langdon, and others of my contemporaries. He would, of course, have developed his style somewhat differently because he wouldn't have had dialogue to enhance his humor. But he does pantomimic skits which are just splendid. He is one of our great pantomimists.

"He has a style different from Chaplin's. Skelton has developed a style that we used to think was risky for a comedian. For example, there's an old rule in the comedy business, as I have already said, that a comedian must not laugh at his own jokes. He must not laugh at himself. You must not let the audience feel that you think you're funny. Because if you do, it usually spoils the humor for them. That's a cardinal rule.

"But Red goes ahead and breaks that rule. He breaks it in a lovely way, however. He laughs at what he does; but he has made his laughter into a gag. It's contagious. It establishes a warm bond between him and the audience. It is just another instance where a great artist is able to break rules and get away with it.

Dick Van Dyke *(top left)* **and Red Skelton** *(bottom left)* **carry forward the comic traditions of the Golden Age of Comedy.**

183

"There are other rules which occasionally can be broken with safety. One is the unwritten law that the comedian must never look into the camera. For him the camera shouldn't exist. He must act as if he didn't know that he was being photographed. And if he looks at the camera, right away he has said to the audience, 'I'm being photographed.'

"But now there are a certain number of comedians who have made it a trick, like the way Skelton laughs at himself, to look into the camera. In other words, we take the audience into our confidence. We look into the camera as if to say, 'Well, what do you know about that!' It is as if he were inviting the audience to talk back. Actually, it is a way of looking into the camera without actually looking into the camera. It is done as a kind of personal characteristic. There is a way of doing it, and if it is not done right, the whole fantasy can be destroyed. Groucho Marx also does this little trick and does it well.

"Red Skelton just loves gags. Nobody in the business loves a gag more than he does. And, what is more, he is excellent on gags. He uses them generally in a broad way. He doesn't use them subtly, as many of us used to, because that's not his character. And, unlike most comedians, he has developed many different characters. Usually, comics stick to one character and are satisfied with the problems that arise from that. Red, on the other hand, is able to handle a number. He may be a little boy. He may become a pompous old senator. He may be a tramp. He becomes many different characters, and he develops them all beautifully. He must study them in order to do this, and he has to analyze them. His comedy is the result of careful study and very hard work. Red knows his comedy; he knows timing and spacing. And he generally knows his lines, too, which is most important."

Another comedian carrying on the most important traditions of film comedy is Dick Van Dyke, the television and motion picture comedian. "Van Dyke is not only an excellent situation actor and comedian," says Lloyd, "he is also a physical comedian in the sense of employing physical gags, body motions, and facial expressions, as well as being an accomplished dancer and semi-acrobat."

184

Such comedians as Dick Van Dyke, Jack Lemmon, Danny Kaye, Peter Sellers, and a number of others are genuine laugh-makers in the Lloyd tradition.

Jack Lemmon has some interesting views of his own. "I think there is a momentary obsession with sex, which I am sure will abate. There is a much wider area than sex for 'legitimate' comedy. Comedy, like drama, must at all times get empathy from the audience through their identification with the characters and with plot situations. Identification with humor comes out of character behavior in these situations. That is what we call legitimate comedy.

"What is missing today in comedy, to a large extent, is visual humor of the Harold Lloyd, Charlie Chaplin, etc., era. There is one simple reason for some of this present-day lack. It is not necessarily a lack of actors capable of performing visual humor, rather, sometimes, it is the high cost entailed in filming this type of comedy. As one example, it often can take days to perfect and film a one minute chase as it appears on the screen.

Harold Lloyd believes that a great comedian must also be a great actor. Two comedians who have taken serious parts successfully in recent years are Ed Wynn and Jackie Gleason.

"Personally, I miss some of the wild, zany, marvelous comedy of that era. It is fascinating to see entire routines that are absolutely unmotivated, but that sustain themselves and are accepted by the audience, purely on their comic worth alone.

"As the theatre audience of America has matured it no longer merely accepts character behavior, no matter what it may be. This [is true] in both drama and comedy. We have to explain why a character behaves in a certain way, and it must be believable. In other words, our drama and comedy may have become more 'honest.' But, sorry to say, our comedy in general has not necessarily remained as funny as in the old days."

In sharp contrast to the comedy of Lemmon, Skelton, or Van Dyke, is a large army of present-day comedians who create laughs in a special restricted way. They are what is known as "stand-up" comedians, laugh-makers who depend mostly upon their verbal jokes and their methods of presenting them. Actually, they are born of television and reflect some of the limitations of that medium.

"They are of a different school," says Lloyd. "It is an entirely different comic procedure. Now, because they have a different way of getting laughs, that doesn't make them less capable. They are, in their own way, great. But I don't think they reflect the multitude of laugh-making techniques that characterized the clowns of the Golden Age of Comedy. I have seen many of the stand-up comedians in night clubs and on the stage as well as on TV. Whether they could carry on their type of performance in a motion picture, where there is a different atmosphere and a different rapport with the audience, I'm not sure.

"I am not a great advocate of the so-called 'sick' comedy. Maybe it is because I belong to the old school—the school that admired the Chaplins and the Keatons and the Fields. I don't claim that my opinion is necessarily the right opinion, and I'm positive I couldn't compete with them at their own medium; but I personally believe that it is the visual type of comedy which implants itself on a person's mind. I have had people who haven't seen my movies for thirty or forty years discuss a visual gag as if they had just seen it the night before. The visual gag stays in the mind. It is a permanent contribution of humor to a person's life.

186

"Sometimes a certain phrase will come out and become very popular. But that will go, and people will turn to something else. However, I found that, as far as my pictures are concerned, there are sequences and visual episodes that have remained as fresh in peoples' minds as if they had just seen them.

"The stand-up comedians—'sick' or 'well'—don't have the advantage of action or thrills or individual sight gags. They have to be content with trying to visualize situations in words. I know how difficult it is to be a stand-up comedian, though it sounds simple. He has to do a tremendous amount of work to get up his routines. For me, the verbal gag will never be as satisfying as the sight gag."

Buster Keaton agrees with Lloyd. "In our day, there was tremendous competition in our field. Today there is none. Jerry Lewis remains on top . . . but Jerry doesn't have Chaplin, Lloyd, Hamilton [Lloyd Hamilton], and a half a dozen others on his heels . . . with Laurel and Hardy coming on apace to reach truly great heights.

"If our comedy is acceptable today," says Keaton, "if the critics rave and the fan letters come in, I think it can be taken for granted that we have contributed to something more than early movies. The laughter of the world?"

Actually, there is plenty of laughter in our country and in the world today. And much of it flows from the performances of our funny men.

While there are numerous current comedians who are following in the great tradition of comedy, nevertheless, the preponderance of films underline horror, sex, crime, brutality. "A story of passion, bloodshed, desire, and death . . . everything, in fact, that makes life worth living," is the text of a movie advertisement appearing in newspapers in 1963. The satire is scarcely apparent amidst the lurid promotion of the day.

Is the humor of a Chaplin or a Sennett a mere nostalgic memory rather than a modern-day necessity?

Watching the passing scene, Harold Lloyd came to the conclusion that an experiment was needed. How would excerpts from some of his famous old films be received today?

He decided he would try to find out.

188

CHAPTER ELEVEN

World of Comedy

Every so often Harold Lloyd showed his films to his children. On one such occasion, his young son asked, "Why don't you show these movies to people of my generation instead of keeping them bottled up the way you are?"

"That started me off," says Harold. "I had presented my film *The Freshman* to an audience in Paris in 1953. My picture *Movie Crazy* had been shown in London some years before that. Their reception had been excellent. Those had been about the only occasions on which I have dusted off my old films and given them a public airing since they were originally released."

But why not reissue them in some form? Lloyd pondered the question. He believed that there was a need for the type of laugh-making that was common in the days of the silent films. But he wasn't sure what the reaction would be if he were to bring his old films back.

He did not want them to fall flat on their faces. They had lived too honorable a life, he thought, to be slighted by a generation for whom they were not made in the first place. Nevertheless, the temptation was strong and friends encouraged him to give it a try.

Harold was, by now, approaching seventy years of age. He has received more than his share of recognition. A few years earlier, the first annual George Eastman Festival of Film Arts in Rochester, New York, had presented gold plaques to ten outstanding stars of the silent films. Among those who were there to accept the awards were Mary Pickford, Lillian Gish, Mae Marsh, Richard Barthelmess, Buster Keaton, and Harold Lloyd. Four other stars, unable to be present, were Norma Talmadge, Gloria Swanson, Ronald Coleman, and Charlie Chaplin.

In 1952, Harold Lloyd was further honored by receiving a special Oscar from the Academy of Motion Picture Arts and Sciences, inscribed, "To Harold Lloyd, master comedian and good citizen."

Lloyd was very conscious of the fact that to most of today's teenagers, and even to many adults, his name meant absolutely nothing. There had been only a few short-run revivals in motion picture houses. Only two of his films had ever appeared on television.

Basically, he didn't like to see his pictures on television, where they are sliced up to fit specific time limits and to make room for commercials. Also the TV screen tends to cut into a film made for a larger showing, sometimes mangling gags and destroying the meaning of an entire sequence. Therefore, he had been extremely reluctant to release them to sponsors; nor had he any particular financial necessity to accept offers made to him.

After wrestling with the problem for a long time and consulting friends whose opinions he valued, Harold Lloyd decided to start the project going. He figured that he could drop it in midstream if he should discover that it would not be of benefit to anyone concerned.

"I found that when I put the first film together and had it shown to certain preview audiences, it appealed to the youth exactly as it had when it was first made, many years before."

It was an eerie feeling for Lloyd. He had been off the screen for twenty years.

"Now, an actor can be off the screen for two years and they can forget him," says Harold. "So if he's been off for twenty years, he's completely forgotten. As far as the younger generation is concerned, I was a nonentity.

"It isn't just a reintroduction. It is a rebirth. It's something like when young Dick Van Dyke, the comedian, first came along a few years ago. No one knew him. Then all of a sudden they discovered him and thought he was funny. That's the

In 1960, Lloyd wondered whether the Harold Lloyd of 1923 could appeal to the new generation.

191

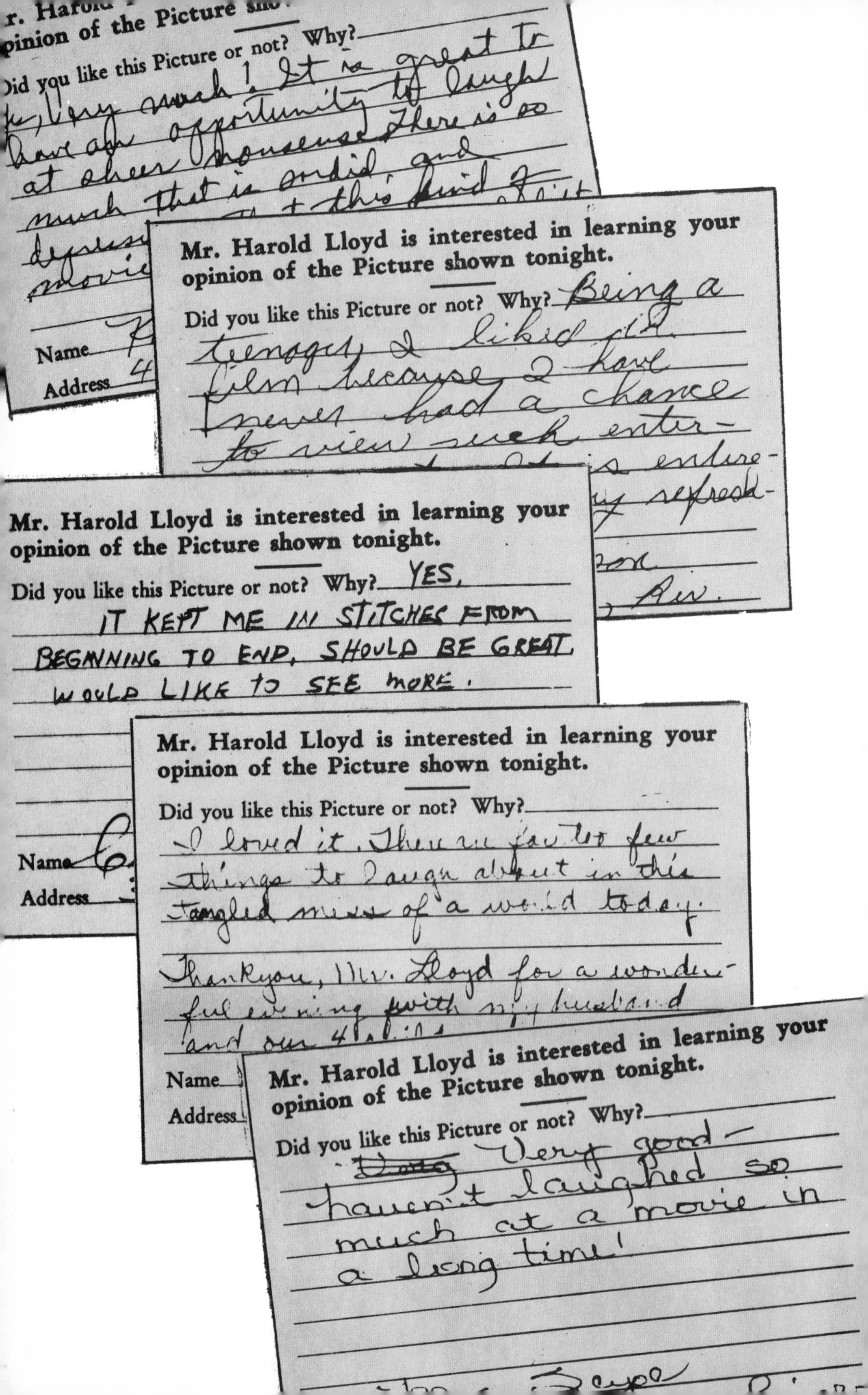

r. Harold [...]
pinion of the Picture sho[...]

Did you like this Picture or not? Why?
[...] very much! It is great to
have an opportunity to laugh
at sheer nonsense. There is so
much that is sordid and
depress[...] [...] this kind of it
movie[...]

Name [...]
Address 4[...]

Mr. Harold Lloyd is interested in learning your opinion of the Picture shown tonight.

Did you like this Picture or not? Why? Being a
teenager I liked it
film because I have
never had a chance
to view such enter-
[...] is entire-
[...] refresh-
[...]
[...] An.

Mr. Harold Lloyd is interested in learning your opinion of the Picture shown tonight.

Did you like this Picture or not? Why? YES,
IT KEPT ME IN STITCHES FROM
BEGINNING TO END, SHOULD BE GREAT,
WOULD LIKE TO SEE MORE.

Name C[...]
Address [...]

Mr. Harold Lloyd is interested in learning your opinion of the Picture shown tonight.

Did you like this Picture or not? Why?
I loved it. There are far too few
things to laugh about in this
tangled mess of a world today.

Thankyou, Mr. Lloyd for a wonderful evening with my husband
and our 4 [...]

Name [...]
Address [...]

Mr. Harold Lloyd is interested in learning your opinion of the Picture shown tonight.

Did you like this Picture or not? Why?
Very good —
haven't laughed so
much at a movie in
a long time!

Harold Lloyd's preview of *World of Comedy* brought many instructive comments from the audience.

way youngsters are. They're always looking for something that's funny. But they have to discover it for themselves. One can't tell them that something is funny because they won't laugh at a reputation; they have to laugh at the gags themselves.

"I'd like to find out whether people will still go to see me," Harold told friends.

So he carefully studied sequences to make up an anthology of some of the most hilarious sections from his old films. He and his co-workers took some twenty-two sequences from his library. Eight were finally selected. To these they added a musical score, sound effects, and subtitles. Independent laugh-provoking incidents were bound together by narrative to make up *Harold Lloyd's World of Comedy.*

Actually Harold had the idea in the back of his head for many years. He wanted to see what the return of his type of comedy, the sight gag, the original situation comedy, would do for a new generation.

The anthology included such famous scenes as the football sequence from *The Freshman;* the famous turkey sequence from *Hot Water;* the new car sequence from *Hot Water;* the Mexican Revolution sequence from *Why Worry?;* the famous boy-girl train sequence from *Girl Shy;* the top-of-the-train sequence from *Professor Beware;* the magician's coat sequence from *Movie Crazy;* and the climbing-up-the-building sequence from *Feet First.* The excerpts dated from the years 1924 to 1938.

"One main problem in screening my type of comedy today," says Harold, "is that audiences have grown too sophisticated to believe in the hair-raising experiences that they see in a movie. They assume it's all a trick. We had to insert a line in the commentary explaining that I performed almost all the stunts myself and that the heights are as high as they appear.

"Kids today, I'm sorry to say, are not familiar with this sort of comedy. I thought perhaps I could start a trend."

In making the picture, Harold Lloyd was fortunate in being able to lean on his old-time associate producer, Jack Murphy, who had remained his aide through the years.

Never one to trust his own opinion without consulting others, Harold organized a "sneak preview," a technique for checking pictures which he had helped to originate in the early days.

"You never know on a movie set whether something will be funny in a theater," he says. "So we always used a sneak preview on our pictures. We really used the preview, not just to confirm our own thinking. If something didn't go right, we went back into production, cutting whole sequences and adding others."

A preview was organized at Bakersfield, California, with an old-time organist playing background music and a packed house of teen-agers as the audience.

At the end of the performance, the young people were asked to fill out cards saying what they thought about the film. The responses were overwhelmingly favorable. "My boy friend laughed continuously . . . the man next to me almost split his sides . . . this was a much finer comedy than nowadays . . . it is clean and humorous . . . today's comedy has too much sex in it . . ."

Of course, there were negative reactions too, and some of the gags which were funny a generation ago somehow failed to arouse much of a response. Nevertheless, the consensus of opinion was hilarity. Harold was encouraged to move ahead.

When the picture itself was presented to the public in America and overseas, nothing the critics said or the public demonstrated was to change Harold's mind.

"What has Hollywood produced lately that compares with half a dozen scenes in that glorious film—as when Lloyd, putting on the magician's dinner jacket by mistake in the men's room at a Hollywood party, returns to the dance floor to find birds, rabbits, and eggs appearing from each pocket and sleeve while he foxtrots with the producer's wife?" asked Arthur Schlesinger, Jr. in *Show* magazine.

"If you've never sat in a crowded theater and rocked with laughter at Harold Lloyd's thrilling antics, then you've missed one of the best treats that movies ever offered," said Joe Franklin in the Denver *Post*.

"It's my guess, nay, prediction, that the young people are going to find the Lloyd revival a rich and glorious experience," said Kaspar Monahan in the Pittsburgh *Press*.

"Lloyd's great sight gags would be slowed up if the action were retarded to match meaningless chatter," said Lyle W. Nash in the Pasadena *Independent*.

"Beneath the pie-in-the-face slapstick is subtle humor, hidden in the perpetual motion, which was a trademark of Lloyd's films," said *Show Business Illustrated*.

"The funniest, side-splittingest thing we've seen in years," said *McCall's* magazine.

"It's thrilling and hilarious, lively and funny. A mad slapstick comedy. Lloyd is a wonderfully appealing comedian of joyous elasticity and boundless inventiveness. A joy and delight in this sad world!" said Bosley Crowther in *The New York Times*.

"Go see it for the laugh of the lifetime," said the *Daily Mirror*.

"My advice is to see it," said the *New York Daily News*.

The reaction abroad was tremendous, too. "The biggest hit of the Cannes Film Festival thus far," commented United Press International, "has been a movie which began forty years ago. And its star, a graying, mild-mannered man who has not made a movie in thirty years, has been wildly cheered by the Festival audiences."

Lloyd recalls how he was met by a lukewarm reception when the idea was suggested of presenting his film to a Cannes Festival audience. "At first, they were completely against it," recalls Harold.

"We came too late. But they said they would look at the picture. They did. Evidently, it had a good reception. It captured them, or charmed them, or whatever term you·think is appropriate. So they agreed to put it on. And it turned out that was the only picture of its kind that they put on that year in the Festival theater."

Harold Lloyd's World of Comedy was not actually entered into the Cannes competition but was shown at an off-hour for those who cared to see it. The theater was jammed with exhibitors, writers, distributors, correspondents, and celebrities of one kind or another from South America, the Orient, India, and all over Europe, as well as the United States.

The reception given to *Harold Lloyd's World of Comedy* was heartwarming to Harold. The picture not only was accompanied by laughter throughout, but, after it was over, Lloyd received a standing ovation.

"It was all the more amazing to me that this international audience enjoyed the picture," said Harold, "in view of the fact

Throughout the world, people eagerly flocked to Harold Lloyd's *World of Comedy* when it was shown in the early 1960's.

196

DE GROOTE KUNSTENAARS VAN HET WITTE DOEK

HAROLD LLOYD

393025A

Paris a retrouvé Harold Lloyd et Capucine

HAROLD LLOYD est arrivé hier à Paris venant de New

เบิกบานบันเทิงไทย

ฉาย ๔ วันที่ ๑ ธันวาคม ๑๑ ค. ๒๕๐๘

ฮาโรลด์ ลอยด์ เตรียมสร้างหนัง

"ตลกเช่นเคยครับ-เร็วๆนี้"

เปิดเผยจากดาราตกก แว่น
ชื่อตัวหนุ่ม ซึ่งเดินทาง มา
เตรียมพบกับนักชม ภาพ-
จีนส์ 'ผมบ้าฟุตบอล'
เตรียม ชอบสร้างหนังพวก นี้ เพราะ
ชวกับ ทำให้คน ดู ได้ทรรศ.คดี
ใหม่ เบิกบานกว่าหนัง ปร เาท
นากาศ อเซียเกรง ยังวงวน กา—
ว่ารวม มารมณ์ ปนไทนไหน"
"

歡迎滑稽大王 夏勞哀 先生蒞港

麗都 盛大獻映 三院 即將

快樂 百老匯

王大稽滑 六經神

夏哀生生表 作代畧先 是利共興 盛 亨別差 的

HAROLD LLOYD

WORLD OF COMEDY

DISTRIBUTED BY COLUMBIA PICTURES

that there was a language barrier. But I shouldn't have been surprised—because humor has always passed over language barriers. It is the one universal language. It's been so long since I have participated in such an event that I had forgotten.

"I was sitting up in the balcony, where they generally put the people who are in the pictures," Harold recalls. "The ovation amazed me. And then they called on me to make a speech. Now I've never been particularly fond of speech-making, and I haven't changed with the years. But the enthusiasm and warmth of the evening moved me deeply.

As he stood up on the box looking at the people, he knew they expected a gag to link him with the picture and his past. The final scene of the movie just witnessed was a young Harold Lloyd doing a fantastic human-fly climbing on the exterior of a building. So an aging Harold Lloyd grabbed hold of the box railing and jumped up on it as if he were going to try another human-fly antic. The audience shrieked. "But I knew better than to do anything drastic. I am not the man I used to be," Harold explained. Doubtless, one reason why the film was so well received was its sharp contrast to so many other films being shown at festivals throughout the world. The Lloyd type of comedy is simply unknown in movie-making today.

The reception abroad for *Harold Lloyd's World of Comedy* was uniformly good. Two theaters in London played the film for sixteen weeks. In Paris, the film was also held for sixteen weeks. In Brussels, it was shown for more than twenty weeks. Tokyo exceeded even this.

Critics abroad, too, were warm in their praise.

"Whether the young people will enjoy the *World of Comedy* I do not know," reported Cassandra, the famed newspaper columnist in the London *Mirror*. "What I do know is that they darn well should."

From the Cannes Film Festival to Bangkok, the reception to Harold Lloyd's film was far beyond his dreams.

In 1964, Lloyd released a second anthology of early pictures entitled *The Funny Side of Life*, which featured his famous feature film *The Freshman*.

198

"It has been amazing to me that these comedies—some of them forty years old—can still strike a responsive note of laughter with audiences of all ages and in all parts of the world.

"Laughter is the universal language," says Harold Lloyd. "It establishes a common identity among people—regardless of other differences. It is the sweetest sound in the whole world."

Some of Harold Lloyd's awards including an Oscar and a Medal of Honor from Lloyd's contemporaries (1915-1925) given through the George Eastman Festival of Film Artists.

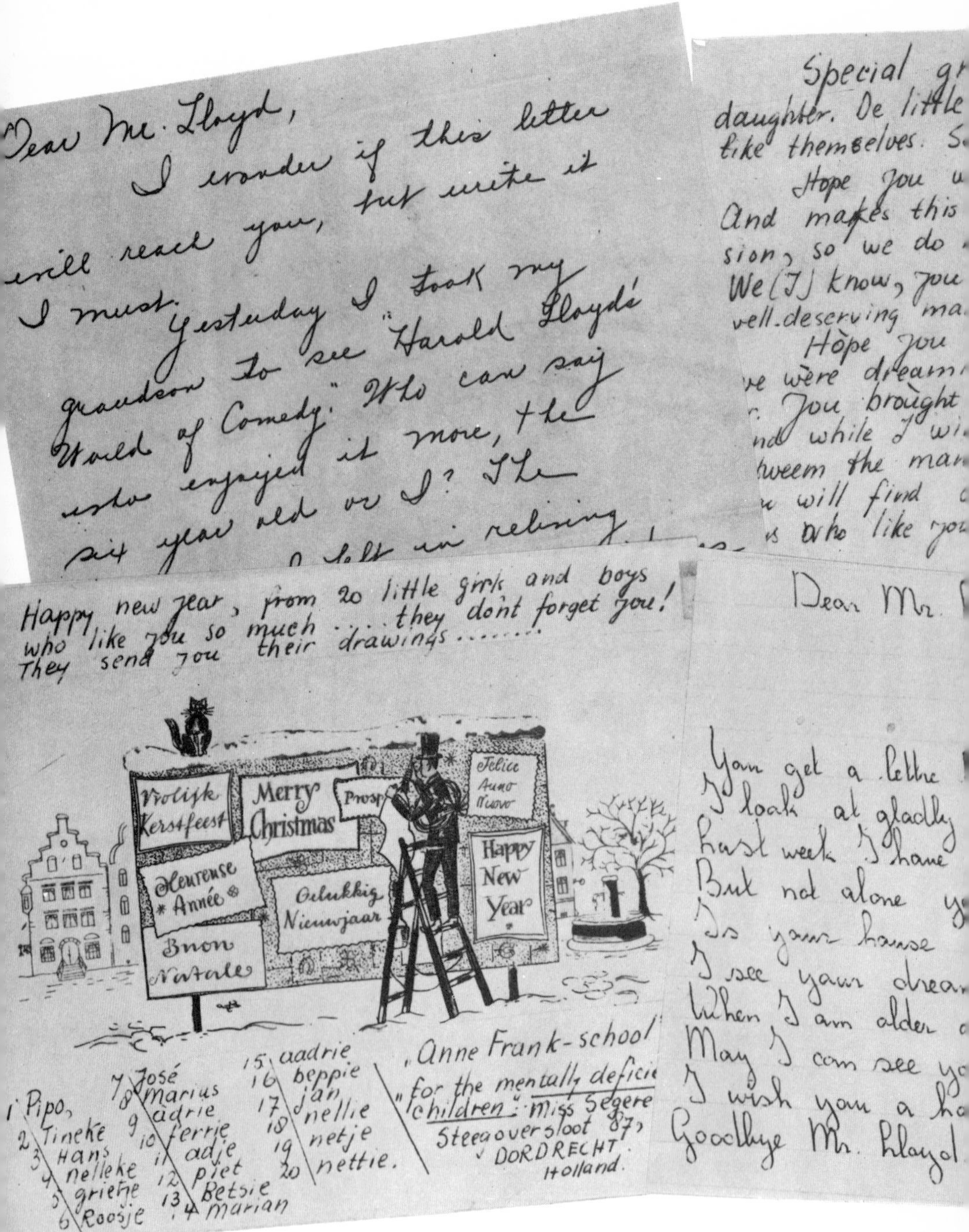

Dear Mr. Lloyd,
I wonder if this letter will reach you, but write it I must.
Yesterday I took my grandson to see "Harold Lloyd's World of Comedy". Who can say who enjoyed it more, the six year old or I? The ... felt in relieving ...

Special gr...
daughter. De little ...
like themselves. S...
Hope you ...
And makes this ...
sion, so we do ...
We (I) know, you ...
vell deserving ma...
Hope you ...
ve were dream...
r. You brought ...
nd while I wi...
hween the man...
u will find ...
s who like you...

Dear Mr. ...

Happy new year, from 20 little girls and boys who like you so much ... they don't forget you! They send you their drawings.........

Vrolijk Kerstfeest
Heureuse Année
Buon Natale
Merry Christmas
Gelukkig Nieuwjaar
Prosp...
Felice Anno Nuovo
Happy New Year

1 Pipo,   7 José   15 aadrie
2 Tineke 8 Marius 16 beppie
3 Hans   9 aadrie 17 jan
4 nelleke 10 ferrie nellie
5 grietje 11 adje   18 netje
6 Roosje 12 piet   19 nettie
          13 Betsie 20
          14 marian

Anne Frank-school
for the mentally deficie...
children: miss Segere...
Steegoversloot 87,
DORDRECHT
Holland.

Dear Mr. ...
You get a lethe ...
I look at gladly ...
Last week I have ...
But not alone y...
is your house ...
I see your dream...
when I am older ...
May I com see yo...
I wish you a ha...
Goodbye Mr. Lloyd...

to your little grand-
think, she is a little-one
love here in their thaug
nderstand.
of letter an unpolite imp
ave the meaning to do so.
a great man, a great
xcuse if we are unpolite.
understand, in our situa
you and your grandda
ness to us. Hope, you lik
disapoint my children
y letters of course you g
a group little girls
from her teacher,
Miss C. M. Segeren,
steegoversloot 87,

INDIANA

Bloomington, Indiana
February 27, 1963

Mr. Harold Lloyd
1225 Benedict Canyon
Beverly Hills,
California

Dear Mr. Lloyd:

I recently had opportunity to see your film and enjoyed it very much. I hope that eventually you might take opportunity to make a new film for the sake of your old and new fans.

I myself am a student at Indiana University and am majoring in history and government, but have long had an amateur interest in the theatre and motion pictures. I believe that the best talent and screen enjoyment came from th...
yoursel...

My Dear Mr. Lloyd,
Although I'm only 13 years old I've been a great admirer of your tremendous contribution to the motion picture industry and have done much research on your entire career.
Your recent compilation of your old films was thoroughly enjoyed by my entire family however, I was positively enthralled. I would be (over)

Holland of a teenager.
ur movies and I fin
ou on the T.V.
ovies but also your
so beautiful and so
always in my dreams.
have money, I am coming to the States.
ause please?
Christmas and a happy New Years

Acknowledgments

We tread on tiptoe when we write about comedy. Just to live dangerously, we occasionally have come down with a heavy foot. But Harold Lloyd, who helped so greatly with this book, is not responsible for its emphases, errors, or omissions. In addition to Mr. Lloyd, we owe a debt to many individuals and organizations, some of whom are listed here. Many more, whose identity is only known to us by the good work they performed, are omitted. For this we are sorry.

My thanks to these individuals and organizations who helped in many ways:

Jack Murphy, New York Public Library Picture Collection; Museum of Modern Art; Buster Keaton; Jack Lemmon; Lucille Ball; Blackhawk Films; French Film Office; *Photography* magazine; United Nations Children's Fund (UNICEF); Brown Brothers; (48,135) Wide World; (173) *Film Quarterly;* New York Public Library Theatre Collection; United Nations Educational, Scientific and Cultural Organization (UNESCO); Hartsook Photographers; (57) London *Mirror* from Gilloon Photo Agency; (8, 16-17) George Eastman House; Ernest F. Hubbard; Columbia Pictures; Associated Press, Joseph Alterman; National Broadcasting Company; Mary McFeely; Eileen Reilly; Continental Distributing, Inc.; Nelson E. Garringer; Uni-William Heinemann, 1951; *W. C. Fields—His Follies and For*-versal Pictures; Metro-Goldwyn-Mayer; RKO; United Artists.

We are indebted also to such authors and publications as the following:

An American Comedy, by Harold Lloyd and Wesley W. Stout, Longmans, Green, 1928; *The Public Arts,* by Gilbert Seldes, Simon and Schuster, 1956; *"Comedy's Greatest Era,"* by James Agee, *Life* magazine, September 15, 1949; *My Wonderful World of Slapstick,* by Buster Keaton and Charles Samuels, Doubleday, 1960; *Life with Groucho,* by Arthur Marx, Popular Library, 1960; *The Marx Brothers,* by Kyle Crichton,

tunes, by Robert Lewis Taylor, Doubleday, 1949; *Father Goose —The Story of Mack Sennett,* by Gene Fowler, Covici-Friede, 1934; *King of Comedy,* by Mack Sennett and Cameron Shipp, Doubleday, 1954; *Charlie Chaplin,* by Theodore Huff, Henry Schuman, 1951; *The Liveliest Art,* by Arthur Knight, Mentor, 1957; *Mr. Laurel and Mr. Hardy,* by John McCabe, Doubleday, 1961; *The Public Is Never Wrong,* by Adolph Zukor, Putnam, 1953.

Beyond Laughter, by Martin Grotjahn, McGraw-Hill, 1957; *Comic Tradition in America,* Kenneth Lynn, editor, Victor Gollancz, 1958; *American Humor,* by Constance Rourke, Doubleday, 1931; *Native American Humour,* by Walter Blair, Chandler, 1960; *Humor in America,* by Max Herzberg and Leon Mones, Appleton-Century-Crofts, 1945; *The Funny Men,* by Steve Allen, Simon and Schuster, 1956; *The Way I See It,* by Eddie Cantor, Prentice-Hall, 1953; *The House That Shadows Built,* by Will Irwin, Doubleday, Doran, 1928; *Native American Humor,* James Aswell, editor, Garden City, 1949; *Easy the Hard Way,* by Joe Pasternak, Putnam, 1956; *From Vaude to Video,* by Abel Green and Joe Laurie, Jr., Henry Holt, 1951; *Classics of the Silent Screen,* by Joe Franklin, Citadel, 1959; *Enjoyment of Laughter,* by Max Eastman, Simon and Schuster, 1936; *Laughter USA,* NBC TV broadcast September 17, 1961, 10-11 p.m., George Burns narration by Richard Hanser and Rod Reed; *50 Years of American Comedy,* by Bill Treadwell, Exposition Press, 1951; *The Fifty Year Decline and Fall of Hollywood,* by Ezra Goodman, MacFadden, 1962; *McGuffey's Fifth Eclectic Reader* (1879 edition), Signet, 1962; *The Film Till Now,* by Paul Rotna; *The Great Stone Face,* by Christopher Bishop, *Film Quarterly,* Fall, 1958; "Classics Revisited— The Gold Rush," by Ernest Callenback, *Film Quarterly,* Summer, 1962; "Harold Lloyd," by Nelson E. Garringer, *Films in Review,* August-September, 1962.

The photographs on Pages 32, 51, 117, 166, and 175 are from the Museum of Modern Art collection. Those on pages 8 and 16-17 are actual pictures of young people enjoying Harold Lloyd's latest motion picture anthology in London. Picture on page 200-201 courtesy of UNICEF by Jack Ling.

Index

206